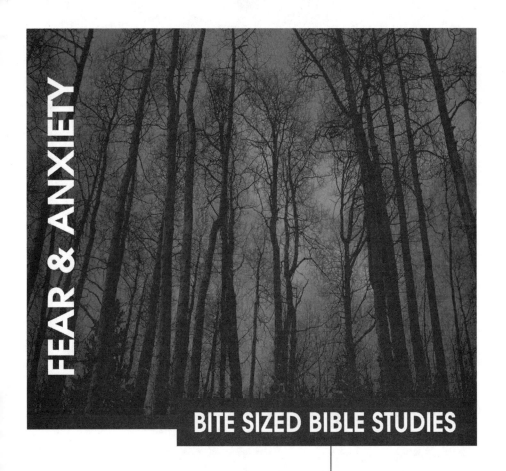

**FEAR & ANXIETY**

**BITE SIZED BIBLE STUDIES**

# Don't Factor Fear Here

*God's Word For Overcoming Anxiety, Fear & Phobias*

6 SESSIONS

**BETH JONES**

*When your words came, I ate them;*
*they were my joy and my heart's delight . . .*
*Jeremiah 15:16 NIV*

## The Bite Sized Bible Study Series Includes . . .

- Satisfied Lives For Desperate Housewives: God's Word On Proverbs 31
- Kissed or Dissed: God's Word For Feeling Rejected & Overlooked
- Grace For The Pace: God's Word For Stressed & Overloaded Lives
- Don't Factor Fear Here: God's Word For Overcoming Anxiety, Fear & Phobias
- The Friends God Sends: God's Word On Friendship & Chick Chat
- What To Do When You Feel Blue: God's Word For Depression & Discouragement

**Beth Jones** is a Bible teacher, author, wife and mother of four children who ministers the Word of God in a relevant and inspiring way by sharing down-to-earth insights. She is the author of the popular Bible study series *Getting A Grip On The Basis* which is being used by thousands of churches in America and abroad, *Why The Gory, Bloody Details?*, and the *Bite Sized Bible Study Series*. Beth also writes a bi-weekly newspaper column titled *"Just Us Girls"* and hosts www.bethjones.org. She and her husband Jeff founded and serve as the senior pastors of Kalamazoo Valley Family Church.

Beth Jones may be reached @
Kalamazoo Valley Family Church, 269.324.5599
www.bethjones.org or www.kvfc.org

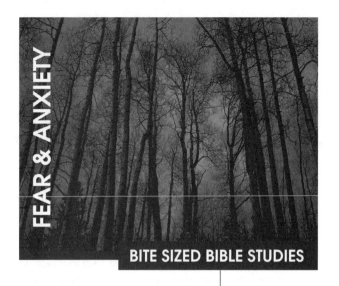

**FEAR & ANXIETY**

**BITE SIZED BIBLE STUDIES**

# Don't Factor
## Fear Here

*God's Word For Overcoming
Anxiety, Fear & Phobias*

6 SESSIONS

**BETH JONES**

Valley Press Publishers
Portage, MI

valleypresspublishers.com

Don't Factor Fear Here
God's Word For Anxiety, Fear & Phobias
ISBN: 1-933433-03-5

Copyright © 2005 Beth Ann Jones

Published by Valley Press Publishers - A Ministry of KVFC
995 Romence Road, Portage, MI 49024
800-596-0379    www.kvfc.org

Printed in the United States of America.
ALL RIGHTS RESERVED.

# Contents

# Acknowledgments

Writing a book is like having a baby! I've been "pregnant" with many books over the years and have found that once a book is "conceived" by the Holy Spirit and begins to grow, the gestation period can range from a few years to several decades. Then it seems that at the right time, when I'm "full-term" and "great with child", the Lord puts an "urge" to write within me which eventually triggers the labor pains, transition and ultimately the birth of a book! It takes a lot of people to give birth to a book and I'd like to honor those the Lord has put in my life to coach, pray, support and encourage me in these writing endeavors.

First, my husband, Jeff. You have been my best friend and most consistent encourager. When I have been uncertain, you've always been rock solid and gone the extra mile to help me fulfill God's will in writing. Thanks for loving me and believing in God's call on my life.

Second, my children, Meghan, Annie, Luke and Eric. I've had to take more time away to write; thanks for being understanding and willing to let mom go. I couldn't have asked for four better children. I love you all.

Third, my mom. What an inspiration you have always been to me! Thanks for letting me hang out with you in Florida to write these books.

Fourth, our staff. Our Associate Publisher, April Wedel, our Editorial Coordinator, Juli DeGraaf and our Publications Coordinator, Joanne Davis. I appreciate your love, faith, heart to get the Word out and the long hours you have spent helping me give birth to this book! I also want to thank the entire KVFC staff for their love, support and encouragement.

Fifth, all the volunteer copy editors and pray-ers. A very special thanks to Mary VanderWal, Carol Lacey and Elise Burch for your time, comments and editing help. I especially appreciate my dear praying friends Mary VanderWal, Mary Jo Fox, Kate Cook, Cindy Boester, Jennifer Nederhoed, Pam Roe-Vanderberg, Jennifer Palthe, Colleen DeBruin, Molly Nicolai, KVFC prayer teams and many others who have continually lifted me and these projects to the Lord in prayer.

Sixth, Pat Judd, Bryan Norris and all the guys with CrossStaff. Thanks for partnering with us in this project. Let's have fun watching what the Lord will do!

I love God's Word. I don't just like it; I love it. It's more valuable to me than anything. If I had to spend the rest of my life on a remote, uninhabited island and could only take one thing, I would take my Bible. Why? It's simple. God has changed and upgraded every area of my life as I have simply read, believed and obeyed the Bible.

It wasn't always that way. Like many people, I had never even considered reading the Bible for myself, much less studying it. The Bible was for priests, theologians and monks. It was not relevant to my life. It was a dusty old book in our basement. One day, when I was about 14 years old, I just got the "urge" to read the Bible. I started with Genesis, and within the first few chapters I fell asleep. That was the end of my Bible reading.

It wasn't until five years later when I was a 19-year-old college freshman that my roommate began to share with me what the Bible said about God, about life and about me. I was shocked at the "living" quality of the Bible. It wasn't like any other book I read. This wasn't like reading the president's biography. This wasn't like reading the dull Western Civilization textbooks in front of me. It was as if God Himself was explaining the contents to me. Something was happening in my heart as I read God's Word. I was challenged. I was encouraged. I was comforted. The Living God was speaking through His Living Word. During this time I developed a hunger for God and His Word. I stayed up late to read the Bible. I pondered it during the day. There was plenty I didn't understand, but I received strength, energy and wisdom just by reading it, and ultimately the Holy Spirit drew me to Jesus.

As a new Christian in my sophomore year of college, my Bible study leader simply exhorted me to read my Bible a lot and "let the Word of Christ dwell richly inside of me." It was the best advice ever! The result was that I began to develop an insatiable appetite for God's Word and a passionate desire to share God's Word with others. As I read my Bible, Jesus walked off the pages and came to live in my heart. Jesus isn't just alive in heaven, He is alive to me. I've come to know Him intimately through fellowship with Him in His Word.

Isn't it great that God's Word is interactive—not just historic or static? God's Word is living and active and able to effectually work within us to affect change and impart the miraculous! The Bible is the most amazing book ever! It has been banned, burned and blasted, but it lives on and continues to be the world's best-selling book.

Unfortunately, I have found that lots of people just don't understand the Bible and as a result, they get overwhelmed, bored or frustrated. Many Christians have never really tasted the rich, daily, life-changing flavor of God's Word. If you want to grow and mature in God, you have to "eat" large quantities of the Word. Once you taste and see that the Lord and His Word are good, nothing else will satisfy you! Think of it this way: if all you've ever tasted are peanut butter and jelly sandwiches, then you are pretty content with a good PBJ. But the minute you taste a filet mignon, you can never again be satisfied by a PBJ. In some ways, I have found that is the story for many Christians. If you're one of those people that have been content with a spiritual PBJ, I've got good news for you; get your taste buds ready for some rich, tasty, "meaty" morsels from God's Word. The more you eat it, the better it tastes!

Our goal in the Bite Sized Bible Study Series is to create an addiction in you for Bible study, and more importantly for knowing God intimately through the revelation knowledge of His Word, by His Spirit. As you explore these studies, I believe that the Holy Spirit will speak to your heart and transmit the supernatural revelation you need to operate victoriously in this life.

Jeremiah was right:

*"When your words came, I ate them;*
*they were my joy and my heart's delight . . ."*
*Jeremiah 15:16, NIV*

May this be your testimony, too!

## How To Use This Bite Sized Bible Study

This Bible study can be used individually as well as in small groups. It's ideal for those who are hungry to learn from the Word, but who have a limited amount of time to meet together with others.

The Bite Sized Bible Study Series is designed for all types of Bible study formats.

- Individual Study
- Women's Small Groups
- Lunchtime Study at Work
- Neighborhood Bible Study
- Couples' Small Groups
- Sunday School Class
- Prison Ministry
- Student and Youth Small Groups
- Outreach Bible Study
- Early Morning Men's Bible Groups
- Singles Small Groups
- Recovery and Felt Need Groups

## For Individual Study

**Pray.** Ask God, by the Holy Spirit, to customize these sessions for you personally.

**Expect.** Turn your "expectation" on and trust God to speak to your heart.

**Dive.** Grab your Bible, pen and favorite beverage and dive in!

# For Small Group Study Leaders

**Pray.** Ask God, by the Holy Spirit, to reveal and customize these sessions for you and your group members.

**Expect.** Turn your "expectation" on and trust God to speak to your heart, as well as the hearts of those in your small group.

**Facilitate.** Small groups will do better with a facilitator, preferably a more mature Christian who can add helpful comments as well as lead a heartfelt time of prayer before and after each session. It's important that you keep things moving in the right direction. As the leader of the small group, keep in mind that it's your job to facilitate discussion and not act as the "teacher" who does all the talking. It's important for those in the group to verbalize their discoveries, so do your best to create an atmosphere where each member feels free to share what they are learning from God's Word.

**Encourage.** Encourage everyone to participate. Help those who talk a lot to take a breather and let others share their insights as well.

**Focus.** Stay focused on God the Father, Jesus, and the Holy Spirit Who gave us the Scriptures. Our goal is to see what God has said in His Word. Keep in mind that this is a Bible study and not a place for "my opinion" or "my church believes" or "here's what I think" comments. Always direct people's attention back to the Bible to see what the Scriptures say.

**Highlight.** Hit the high points. If you face time constraints, you may not have enough time to cover every detail of each lesson. As the leader, prayerfully prepare and be sure you cover the highlights of each session.

**Digest.** We've endeavored to "cut up" the Word through this Bite Sized Bible Study, and as a leader it's your job to help those in your small group digest the Scriptures so they can benefit from all the spiritual nutrition in each word.

**Discuss.** Take time to answer the three discussion questions at the end of each Bible study session. These should help stimulate heartfelt conversation.

If you want this Bible study to really impact your life, you must be certain of one major thing: you must be certain you are a Christian according to God's definition and instruction in the Bible. You must be certain that you are accepted by God; that you are saved. So let's begin our study by considering this important issue.

Did you know that some people want to be a Christian on their terms, rather than on God's terms? Sometimes people want to emphasize church, religion and their goodness as evidence of their Christianity. For some, it will be a rude awakening to discover that the Bible tells us God isn't impressed by any of those substitutes. Did you know that God isn't interested in our denominational tags? He's not wowed by our church membership pedigree, either. He's not moved by our good deeds and benevolent accomplishments. The thing that most impresses God is His Son, Jesus Christ. *"For God so loved the world that he gave his one and only Son, that whoever believes in him shall not perish but have eternal life."* John 3:16, NIV God paid quite a price to send His own Son to the cross to pay the penalty for our sin. It's really an insult to Him to trust in or substitute any thing or anyone else for Jesus Christ. The key to being a Christian is to believe in, trust in, receive and confess Jesus Christ as your Lord and Savior.

Why would you or anyone want to believe in, trust, receive and confess Jesus Christ as Lord? Why would you want to know Jesus personally and to be known by Him? Unless you truly understand your condition before God, you wouldn't have any reason to! However, when you realize the magnitude of your sin—those private and public thoughts, deeds, actions and words that you and God know about—when you listen to your conscience and realize that truly "all have sinned," including you, it can be very sobering. It's even more sobering to realize that according to God's justice system, *". . . the wages of sin is death . . ."* Romans 6:23 NKJV. It's a big wake up call when it really hits you that the consequence of sin is death. Death which is defined as an eternal separation from God is the payment you will receive for your sin. When you realize your true, hopeless, lost condition before God, you will run to Him in order to be saved. This reality causes people to quit playing religious games and to quit trusting in their own works of righteousness. Our lost condition forces us to forgo being "churchy" or "religious", apathetic, passive and indifferent, and to become hungry for the Merciful Living God. It's good news to discover that " . . . *the gift of God is eternal life in Christ Jesus our Lord." Romans 6:23 NKJV*

What does God require of us? The qualification for eternal life is simply to believe on Jesus. Many people say they believe in God or in Jesus Christ. In fact, the Bible tells us that the devil himself believes and trembles. According to the Bible, God's definition of a Christian believer—or a Christ One—is the person who believes in their heart that God raised Jesus from the dead and who confesses with his or her mouth that Jesus Christ is their Lord. In other words, their heart and mouth agree that Jesus is Lord! We see this in Romans 10:13, 9, ". . . *whoever calls on the name of the LORD shall be saved . . . if you confess with your mouth the Lord Jesus and believe in your heart that God has raised Him from the dead, you will be saved." NKJV*

This is something we do on purpose. It's a sobering thought to consider that if you've never purposely repented of your sin and invited Jesus Christ to be the Lord of your life, you may not be saved—you may not be a Christian according to God's definition. Would you like to be certain that you are a Christian; that you have a relationship with the Lord and eternal salvation? It's simple, just answer these questions: Do you believe that God raised Jesus from the dead? Will you give Him the steering wheel of your life and trust Him to forgive all your sins and make you an entirely new person? Will you trust Jesus Christ alone to save you? Are you willing to invite Him into your life and will you confess that He is your Lord? If so, please pray this prayer from your heart. God will hear you, Jesus Christ will forgive your sins and enter your life. You will be a Christian.

*"Dear God, I come to you as a person who recognizes my condition before you. I see that I am a sinner in need of a Savior. Jesus, I do believe that God raised You from the dead and I now invite you into my life. I confess Jesus as my Lord. I want to know You and be the Christian You have called me to be, according to Your definition. I thank You, in Jesus' Name. Amen."*

The popular TV show *Fear Factor* has hit a nerve with America! Young, buff people walk thirty stories above the ground on beams of steel, hang from helicopters over swamps, lie in glass cages while spiders and snakes crawl over their faces, they drink blended roaches, cow eyeballs and worms, not to mention other horrendous animal body parts. The TV audience gets an adrenaline rush just watching. It's gross! It's addictive. Millions of viewers tune in every week to watch these people defy their greatest fears. Who knows how long this craze to watch others overcome their fears will last?

The climbing wall was a new attraction at our annual church Halloween-alternative party. How hard could it be, I wondered? I thought I was pretty tough as I strapped into the climbing wall harness. All I have to do is grip the little rubber thingies, start climbing and ring the bell, right? No problem! While I was getting buckled in, I noticed my kids and dozens of other children gathered around the wall to watch Mom—aka, one of the pastors—climb the wall. Soon, I heard other moms standing by and cheering me on. It hit me, *"Oh no, now I have an audience and I have to do this! I have to get to the top and ring that stupid bell!"* I double-checked the harness to be sure every thread was intact, and feeling confident I began the climb. The first six steps were a cinch. I was just a little more than half-way up the wall when it hit me: fear! Suddenly, I froze. I could feel my legs shaking. I didn't move. I just clung to the wall, gripped with fear. Looking down wasn't good, and when I looked up at the bell it seemed to be a mile away. The next step seemed farther away than the previous ones, and the grips seemed to be getting smaller. I wrestled within myself, *"I can't do it. I don't want to do it. I want to go home now . . . but, I can't be a wimp. What do I do?"* I was still frozen and basically velcroed to the climbing wall; I did not want to move. I could hear my kids down below, *"C'mon Mom, you can do it."* I heard the other moms cheering. Suddenly, I heard the man holding my harness ropes from below. *"I've got you ma'am,"* he said, as he gave a gentle tug on the rope to let me know that indeed, my life was in his hands. I started to move one leg up as if I would try to take the next step, when the man holding the harness gave me a stronger tug and actually helped to lift me to the next grip. When I felt him tugging on that rope and helping to pull me up that climbing wall, I realized that someone stronger than me was holding me up. I felt a sense of peace and comfort, and I was energized to finish the climb. The man holding the rope "pulled" me up the entire way as I moved to the top. Finally, I rang the bell! I was quite happy it was over, and equally happy that I had overcome my fear to ring the bell. No one but me and the "harness man" knew the real story. It was only knowing he was holding me up that gave me the confidence and peace to finish the climb.

## He's Got You!

How true this is in our lives!! Sometimes when we look at the walls in front of us, it can look scary. When we realize that the Lord God Almighty loves us, has a tight grip on the rope and gently pulls us up to victory after victory, we can relax in His care, free from fear. It's my prayer that as you study these sessions you hear the Holy Spirit say, *"I've got you ma'am"* or *"I've got you sir."*

Anxiety, phobias, worry, nervousness, being scared, freaking out, and full blown panic . . . many people struggle with these things to various degrees. Sometimes there are mental, emotional issues, chemical imbalances in our bodies, toxins and allergens from our diet and a host of other natural causes that can incite anxiety and fear. Sexual, physical, mental and spiritual abuse can keep a person bound in fear. A special class of anti-anxiety drugs has been created to help people function in peace; free from panic. People are afraid to die and they are afraid to live. People who live in obsessive-compulsive behavior patterns often suffer from a root of fear. If you are frustrated and worn out from fear, I have good news for you! Fear does not have to be a factor for you! You don't have to factor fear here! Jesus told us so!

Jesus said it over and over: *"Fear not. Be not afraid. Don't be anxious. Don't worry about your life."* Is this possible? In a world of danger, evil and calamity, is it possible to live free from fear? Yes, it is, and that's the focus of this entire Bite Sized Bible Study. We'll be looking at some of the most common fears and some of the most important factors to overcoming anxiety, fear and phobias.

Before we begin, perhaps it would be helpful to locate the areas the enemy has worked fear into your life and start believing God now for complete freedom from fear. Expect peace, courage, faith and love to replace all your fears!

## Are You Afraid, Anxious or Phobic?

Which, if any, of these statements apply to your life?

___ I worry a lot.

___ I have frequent anxiety or panic attacks.

___ The news makes me fearful.

___ I am afraid of the future.

___ I have a social phobia.

___ I am nervous a lot.

___ I usually expect the worst.

___ I am afraid for my children's safety.

___ I worry that my spouse will have an affair.

___ I am afraid for my own safety.

___ I fear change.

___ I live in fear because of past experiences in my life.

___ Fear has held me back from opportunities for fun and success.

___ I am afraid to die.

___ I am anxious about driving, flying, speaking or heights.

___ I am afraid of snakes, spiders, worms or other creeping animals.

___ I am obsessive-compulsive in areas of my life.

___ I struggle with addictions.

___ I worry that my children will not succeed in school, relationships or life.

___ I am afraid that we won't have enough money for bills, college or vacation.

___ I worry that my house is not clean enough.

Here's a partial list of phobias.[1] Circle any of these phobias that apply to you. Be encouraged Jesus wants to deliver us from all our fears!

*Ablutophobia- Fear of washing or bathing.*
*Achluophobia- Fear of darkness.*
*Acrophobia- Fear of heights.*
*Agateophobia- Fear of insanity.*
*Agraphobia- Fear of sexual abuse.*
*Ailurophobia- Fear of cats.*
*Altophobia- Fear of heights.*
*Androphobia- Fear of men.*
*Anthropophobia- Fear of people or society.*
*Anuptaphobia- Fear of staying single.*
*Arachibutyrophobia- Fear of peanut butter sticking to the roof of the mouth.*
*Arachnephobia or Arachnophobia- Fear of spiders.*
*Arithmophobia- Fear of numbers.*
*Aviophobia or Aviatophobia- Fear of flying.*
*Bibliophobia- Fear of books.*
*Cacophobia- Fear of ugliness.*
*Caligynephobia- Fear of beautiful women.*

*Cancerophobia or Carcinophobia- Fear of cancer.*
*Claustrophobia- Fear of confined spaces.*
*Dentophobia- Fear of dentists.*
*Didaskaleinophobia- Fear of going to school. (Got any kids with this one?)*
*Ecclesiophobia- Fear of church. (We know lots of people with that one!)*
*Eisoptrophobia- Fear of mirrors or of seeing oneself in a mirror.*
*Ephebiphobia- Fear of teenagers.*
*Gamophobia- Fear of marriage.*
*Geliophobia- Fear of laughter.*
*Genophobia- Fear of sex.*
*Gerascophobia- Fear of growing old.*
*Glossophobia- Fear of speaking in public or of trying to speak.*
*Hemophobia or Hemaphobia or Hematophobia- Fear of blood.*
*Hippopotomonstrosesquippedaliophobia- Fear of long words.*
*Homilophobia- Fear of sermons. (Know anyone with this?)*
*Homophobia- Fear of homosexuality or of becoming homosexual.*
*Levophobia- Fear of things to the left side of the body.*
*Lilapsophobia- Fear of tornadoes and hurricanes.*
*Linonophobia- Fear of string.*
*Mageirocophobia- Fear of cooking. (I think I'll use this one!)*
*Metrophobia- Fear or hatred of poetry.*
*Misophobia or Mysophobia- Fear of being contaminated with dirt or germs.*
*Novercaphobia- Fear of your step-mother.*
*Octophobia - Fear of the figure 8.*
*Papaphobia- Fear of the Pope.*
*Pentheraphobia- Fear of mother-in-law.*
*Phobophobia- Fear of phobias.*
*Phronemophobia- Fear of thinking.*
*Pyngenesophobia- Fear of relatives.*
*Technophobia- Fear of technology.*

Perhaps the worst fear is the fear of fear! As President Roosevelt once said, *"the greatest thing we have to fear is fear itself."* The enemy uses the vehicle of "lies" to throw people into the fear of fear and the paralyzing cycle it creates.

Regardless of the cause or root, God doesn't want His children in bondage to the paralyzing effects of anxiety, fear or phobias. He's given us compassionate, practical help in the Bible, so let's take a journey and discover what God has revealed in His Word about freedom from fear.

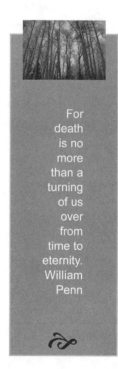

# Fear Of Death

A British statesman once asked his young nephew this question, *"Son, what do you want to be when you grow up?"*
His nephew replied, *"First I want to go to college."*
*"Then what?"* asked the uncle.
"Then, I want to be a lawyer." *"Then what?"*
"Then I want to get married," said the nephew.
*"Then what?"* "Then, I want to have children and raise a family."
*"Then what?"* "Then, I want to retire." *"Then what?"*
"Then I want to travel the world," replied the nephew.
*"Then what?"*
"Then, I guess I'll die," said the nephew.
*"Then what?"*

Have you thought about your "after life"? After *you* die, then what? Diana Ross sang the classic question, *"Do you know where you're going to?"* It's a big question we need to consider. When our bodies are *six feet under*, where will the "*real us*" be? I want to start this Bible study by looking at the greatest fear of all: the fear of death. Once you get the victory in this area, the other areas of anxiety, fear and phobias are much easier to overcome. So, let's ask some basic questions.

Are you afraid to die? Some people freely admit they fear life after death. They don't know where they are going and they are afraid to die. Other people shrug their shoulders and say they are not the least bit afraid of death. At least, that's what they say, but often the reason they make that statement is because they have never really been honest

> For death is no more than a turning of us over from time to eternity. William Penn

enough to give any thought to life beyond death. The very thought of eternity scares them and they avoid thinking about their own mortality, thus in a *"hear no evil, see no evil"* kind of way they have insulated themselves from the idea of death entirely. Still others are quick to confirm that they are not afraid to die because Jesus Christ is their Lord and Savior, and they have complete confidence they will spend their eternal life with Him.

So, what about it? Is there anything after this life? When you're dead, is that it, life is over? Is death the end or the beginning? Can you know where you will go after you die or is life after death just one of life's great uncertainties?

## Ideas People Have About Life After Death

People have come up with all kinds of unbiblical ideas about life after death. Some people teach that once we die we cease to exist. They say that once we are gone, that's it. There is no life after this one. Others believe in reincarnation; that there are several lives after this life. That is, once we die, we may come back to earth as another human being or perhaps an animal. Still, others teach that we move on to different levels of spirituality in life after death. There are those who don't believe in a place called hell, but rather they are convinced that a "loving God" will send everyone to heaven after death. Others do believe in hell and they plan to go there and *"party with all their friends."* There are entire radical groups that base the motivation for their cause on their hope of afterlife pleasures; they believe that those who commit homicide/suicide missions in the name of the cause will be rewarded in heaven with an eternity of virgins when they die. People have all sorts of hopes for life after death.

John Lennon, one of the famous Beatles, rejected religion and dogma, but he was not really an atheist—he espoused a sort of vague spirituality. In the song "Imagine", he wrote: *"Imagine there's no heaven, It's easy if you try, No hell below us, Above us only sky, imagine all the people Living for today . . . Imagine there's no countries, It isn't hard to do, Nothing to kill or die for, No religion too."*

In an effort to find comfort, people come up with reasons for the death of a loved one and their notions of afterlife. Perhaps you've heard grieving people say things like, once a person dies they become one of God's angels, or after a person dies they become a petal in God's garden. Maybe you've heard people say that God took someone to heaven because He was lonely or He needed them in heaven more than we needed them on earth.

Listen to what several historical figures people have on their deathbed.

*I'm bored with it all.*
*(Before slipping into a coma. He died 9 days later.)*
*Winston Churchill, statesman, d. January 24, 1965*

*Damn it . . . Don't you dare ask God to help me.*
*(To her housekeeper, who had begun to pray aloud.)*
*Joan Crawford, actress, d. May 10, 1977*

*I am not the least afraid to die.*
*Charles Darwin, d. April 19, 1882*

*A King should die standing.*
*Louis XVIII, King of France, d. 1824*

*Go on, get out - last words are for fools who haven't said enough.*
*(To his housekeeper, who urged him to tell her his last words*
*so she could write them down for posterity.)*
*Karl Marx, revolutionary, d. 1883*

*Nothing matters. Nothing matters.*
*Louis B. Mayer, film producer, d. October 29, 1957*

*Lord help my poor soul.*

*Edgar Allan Poe, writer, d. October 7, 1849*


*I have offended God and mankind*

*because my work did not reach the quality it should have.*

*Leonardo da Vinci, artist, d. 1519*


*I die hard but am not afraid to go.*

*George Washington, US President, d. December 14, 1799*


*I am ready.*

*Woodrow Wilson, US President, d. 1924*


*I cannot believe in the immortality of the soul . . . No, all this talk of an*

*existence for us, as individuals, beyond the grave is wrong. It is born of our*

*tenacity of life – our desire to go on living . . . our dread of coming to an end.*

*Thomas Edison, American inventor (1847-1931).*


*Speculations! I know nothing about speculations. I'm resting on certainties.*

*I know that my redeemer liveth, and because He lives, I shall live also.*

*(When journalists questioned him as to his speculations about life after death.)*

*Sir Michael Faraday, great Christian and scientist*


*Live in Christ, live in Christ, and the flesh need not fear death.*

*John Knox*


*The best of all is, God is with us. Farewell! Farewell!*

*(On his death bed.)*

*John Wesley*

*I shall be satisfied with thy likeness — satisfied, satisfied!*

*(On his death bed.)*

Charles Wesley

What does God say about afterlife? Men and women have lots of theories, but has God told us anything definitive in His Word? Yes, He has! Let's look at it.

The Bible says, *"It is appointed unto men once to die, but after this the judgment."* Hebrews 9:27 In other words, the Bible tells us that we die once (not two or three times) and when we die, we have to face a judgment.

If death were the end of existence, why would we face judgment? Apparently, after we die physically, we are still alive! The "real us" is still alive once our bodies die. If that is true, are you ready to stand before God Almighty?

## One Thing Is Certain

The thing we know for sure is this: 100% of us will die. In his book *Beyond Death's Door*, cardiologist Dr. Maurice Rawlings shares stories from his own personal experience in resuscitating patients from clinical death.[1] These patients recount their deathbed experiences and help to answer such questions as: Does death represent the end of this life or the beginning of another? Is there evidence to support the biblical descriptions of hell? There are chilling stories of these after-life encounters that include people descending into a place they called hell.

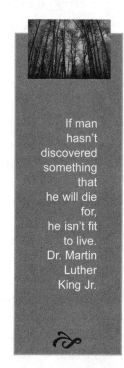

If man hasn't discovered something that he will die for, he isn't fit to live.
Dr. Martin Luther King Jr.

Here's what he said: *"More and more of my patients who are recovering from serious illnesses tell me there is life after death. There is a heaven and a hell. I had always thought death as painless extinction. I had bet my life on it. Now I have had to reconsider my own destiny, and what I have found isn't good. I have found it really may not be safe to die! The turning point in my own thinking occurred because . . . I requested that a patient perform what we call a "stress test" to evaluate complaints of chest pains . . . This patient was a forty-eight-year-old white male who was a rural carrier . . . Unfortunately, he represented one of those rare instances where the EKG not only went "haywire," but the heart stopped altogether, He had a cardiac arrest and dropped dead right in my office . . . While I started external heart massage by pushing on his chest, one nurse initiated mouth-to-mouth breathing. Another nurse found a breathing mask, another nurse brought the emergency cart containing pacemaker equipment. Unfortunately, the heart would not maintain its own beat. A complete heart block had occurred . . . I had to insert a pacemaker . . . the patient began "coming to". . . Each time he regained heartbeat and respiration, the patient screamed, "I am in hell!" He was terrified and pleaded with me to help him. I was scared to death. In fact, this episode literally scared the hell out of me! He then issued a very strange plea: "Don't stop!" . . . Then I noticed a genuinely alarmed look on his face. He had a terrified look worse than the expression seen in death. This patient had a grotesque grimace expressing sheer horror! His pupils were dilated, and he was perspiring and trembling . . . He said, "Don't you understand? I am in hell. Each time you quit I go back to hell! Don't let me go back to hell!" . . . By this time the patient had experienced three or four episodes of complete unconsciousness and clinical death from cessation of both heartbeat and breathing . . . he finally asked me, "How do I stay out of hell?" I told him I guessed it was the same principle learned in Sunday school- that I guessed Jesus Christ would be the one whom you would ask to save you. Then he said, "I don't know how. Pray for me." Pray for him! What nerve I told him I was a doctor, not a preacher. "Pray for me!" he repeated. I knew I had no choice . . . So I had him repeat the words after me as we worked-right there on the floor. It was a very simple prayer because I did not know much about praying. It went something like this: Lord Jesus, I ask you to keep me out of hell. Forgive my sins. I turn my life over to you. If I die, I want to go to heaven. If I live, I'll be "on the hook" forever. The patient's condition finally stabilized, and he was transported to a hospital. I went home, dusted off the Bible and started reading it.*

Interesting, isn't it? Sobering, too. What does the Bible tell us about eternity, beyond death's door? Can we be free from the fear of death? On what do we base our belief concerning the afterlife? There is only one source of truth—God's Word. Let's look at this subject.

1.      Hebrews 2:14-15

Underline the phrase "those who lived all their lives as slaves to the fear of dying."

*14 Because God's children are human beings — made of flesh and blood — Jesus also became flesh and blood by being born in human form. For only as a human being could he die, and only by dying could he break the power of the Devil, who had the power of death. 15 Only in this way could he deliver those who have lived all their lives as slaves to the fear of dying. NLT*

*14 Inasmuch then as the children have partaken of flesh and blood, He Himself likewise shared in the same, that through death He might destroy him who had the power of death, that is, the devil, 15 and release those who through fear of death were all their lifetime subject to bondage. NKJV*

Who is behind the "fear of death"? __the devil__

What does the fear of death do to us? __keeps us from trusting God & living fullest life possible__

Often people don't want to talk about death, yet the Bible tells us that whether people admit it or not and whether they talk about it or not, everyone is afraid to die. *release fear of death*

Jesus died so that we could experience what? __eternal life__

**Nugget** As a six-year-old girl, I distinctly remember being absolutely afraid to die. My sisters and I would lie in bed and talk about where we would spend forever. I couldn't imagine how long forever was and I tried to get to the end of eternity in my mind, but obviously couldn't get there. Then I would think, *"Where will I be? Will I be in the ground? Will my body rot? Will worms get me?"* It was morbid, but that is what my six-year-old mind was wondering. Unfortunately, at the time my parents didn't know what to tell me to give me assurance about life after death, so I lived with this subconscious fear of death until I was 19 years old. I had been afraid to die from 1959 until 1978, but in 1978 I was set free from the fear of death. The secret was that I discovered what Jesus said about life after death—being saved or "born-again". When I invited Jesus Christ to be the Lord of my life, I received freedom from the fear of death, and from that point on I have known Him and have the assurance that when I die, I will spend eternity with God in heaven.

2.        Psalm 23:4

Underline the phrases "the valley of the shadow of death" and "I will fear no evil."

*Even though I walk through the valley of the shadow of death, I will fear no evil, for you are with me; your rod and your staff, they comfort me. NIV*

How do you describe a shadow?  *always with you*

What do you think it means to "walk through" the valley of the shadow of death?

*Come to the other side*

When fear tries to cast the long shadow of death, what is our response supposed to be?

*Fear no evil for God is with us always*

Why can we have this response?  *We are comforted*

# Neutralize The Fear Of Death

Often the fear of death is the root of all fear. If we can neutralize this ultimate fear, then we will find peace, courage and faith in other arenas of life where fear, anxiety, panic and phobias have tried to take hold.

1.      Revelation 12:10-11

Underline the last sentence of this passage.

*10 Then I heard a loud voice shouting across the heavens, "It has happened at last — the salvation and power and kingdom of our God, and the authority of his Christ! For the Accuser has been thrown down to earth — the one who accused our brothers and sisters before our God day and night. 11 And they have defeated him because of the blood of the Lamb and because of their testimony. And they were not afraid to die. NLT*

What three things defeat the devil, the accuser?

*Salvation, power, kingdom of God*

*Authority of Christ*

*Blood of the Lamb*

&Nugget& This is an interesting passage because often believers are aware that the Blood of Jesus and the word of our testimony are powerful weapons against devil's work, but many times we do not realize the power of being free from the fear of death. The fear of death is one of satan's tools for paralyzing people. When we are not afraid to die, he cannot use that fear against us. If we want to neutralize the fear of death, we need to get to the place where we truly do not fear death.

To die will be an awfully big adventure. Aristotle

Are you afraid to die? _Sometimes_

Would you like to know how to overcome this fear? _Yes_

God wants us to be free from the fear of death. Jesus died on the cross to take our place; these are words that we've heard for many years, yet it's true. It's the Great Exchange! Jesus died on the cross and took our place in death, so that we could receive His gift of eternal life. Jesus did His part, and now it's up to us to receive Him and the work that He did.

2.      1 John 5:11-13

Underline verse 12.

*11 And this is the testimony: that God has given us eternal life, and this life is in His Son. 12 He who has the Son has life; he who does not have the Son of God does not have life. 13 These things I have written to you who believe in the name of the Son of God, that you may know that you have eternal life, and that you may continue to believe in the name of the Son of God. NKJV*

What do we know for sure God has given us, according to verse 11?

_Eternal life in His Son_

If you have the Son, Jesus, what do you know you have? _Eternal life_

If you do not have the Son, Jesus, what do you know that you do not have?

_Eternal life_

If you believe in the name of the Son of God, Jesus, what do you know you have?

_Eternal life_

How do you define the word "know"? *Believe – assured*

It's great news to know you have eternal life! The day you receive Jesus Christ and "have the Son" is a day of liberty! You discover freedom from the fear of death that held you in a subtle bondage all your life! If you've received and believed in Jesus as your Lord, you can know for certain you have eternal life and the fear of death is vanquished! When we die and leave these earthly bodies of ours, the real us will go to be with the Lord. If you have not yet received Jesus as your Lord, we will take time to pray and invite Jesus into your life at the conclusion of this lesson.

3.      2 Corinthians 5:6-8

Underline where we will be after we die.

*6 Now we look forward with confidence to our heavenly bodies, realizing that every moment we spend in these earthly bodies is time spent away from our eternal home in heaven with Jesus. 7 We know these things are true by believing, not by seeing. 8 And we are not afraid but are quite content to die, for then we will be at home with the Lord. TLB*

While we are alive on Planet Earth in our earthly bodies, we are physically absent from the Lord. When we leave these earthly bodies, where will we be?

*Present with God*

What are we not to fear? *Dying*

☙**Nugget**☙ When you think about it, our real home is in heaven. That's where we will spend the majority of our existence! We may live on Earth for several decades, but we will spend eternal decades with the Lord in heaven. Our 70, 80, 90 or more years on Earth are a flash in the pan compared to living for billions and billions of years in heaven! We are citizens of heaven, and we are just pilgrims here for a short season.

Actually, the Bible says that we are ambassadors for Christ here on Earth. We are on assignment. This is not our "mother country," but this is where we are assigned for a space of time to proclaim freedom in Christ. We need to think more like an ambassador and less like a native!

We need to consider our life on Earth much like a short vacation . . . that is, don't unpack! Live out of your suitcase! There is something temporary about living from your suitcase. You know that your real home isn't here. When you know where your home is, when you think about sleeping in your own bed, eating out of your own refrigerator and getting home, it makes it easy to temporarily live out of your suitcase. This is the reality for a believer. Heaven is our home and we are living out of our suitcase for now!

## Freedom From The Fear Of Death

Understanding things to come and knowing what the Bible says about our future can bring us out of bondage into freedom from the fear of death.

1.      Hebrews 9:27

Underline the word that describes how many times we die.

*And as it is appointed for men to die once, but after this the judgment.*
*NKJV*

It is certain that 100% of us will die someday. What else is 100% certain?

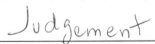
Judgement

&Nugget& If you are a believer in Jesus this is great news, because you know that your sins were already judged when Jesus took them to the cross on your behalf. It's wonderful to know that Jesus truly died to take away my sins! As a believer, you don't fear judgment, but rather look forward to the day when you stand before God the Father, look over at Jesus and hear Him say, *"Father, I took their sin on the cross and washed them in my blood. They believe, trust and have received*

*Me to be their Lord and Savior. Their penalty has been paid. They have passed from death to life."* What a joy it will be to hear the Father say, *"Enter into the joy of the Lord."*

≈**Nugget**≈ On the other hand, if you are an unbeliever, you *should* be afraid to die! I'm not saying that as a fear tactic, it's a reality. If you do not have the Son, Jesus Christ, you do have something to be legitimately afraid of. You have not passed from death to life, but rather are still dead in your sins. When you stand before God you will have to give an account of your life and deeds, and if you have committed one sin then you will have to pay the penalty of eternal death yourself. If you have rejected the price that God paid for your sin, the blood of His Son, then you will have to pay it yourself and the Bible says the *"wages of sin is death."* Romans 3:23 You'll have to pay for your own sin with death, which is an eternal separation from God in a place called hell. If I was an unbeliever, I'd be shaking in my boots! The fear of death is valid for you. If Jesus is not your Lord, then your life on Earth is as good as it gets for you because there is a severe judgment coming your way. The final penalty will be eternity in hell and the lake of fire. It's terrifying. The Bible has a lot to say about this place of torment and you don't want to go there!

≈**Nugget**≈ Sometimes people wonder, *"How could a loving God send anyone to hell?"* Hell is described in the Bible as a place of torment and torture, death and darkness, worms and wailing, grotesqueness and gnashing of teeth; not a place you want to be, ever, let alone forever! (Read Revelations 20:11-15, Luke 12:5, Luke 16:19-31) The truth is God doesn't *send* anyone to hell, but He does allow us the free will to choose hell when we reject His Son, Jesus Christ. God doesn't want anyone to go to hell. That is why He sent His Son, so that none of His children would have to spend eternity in the place that was originally prepared for the devil and his demons. Nevertheless, God allows us to have a free will, and if we choose to remain separated from God through sin and rejecting His Son, Jesus Christ. He'll let us. It's not His desire, but He loves us enough to allow us to have a free will.

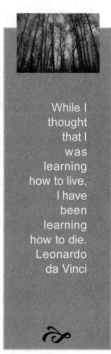

While I thought that I was learning how to live, I have been learning how to die.
Leonardo da Vinci

2.　　John 3:16

Underline the phrase "not perish" and "have everlasting life."

*For God so loved the world that He gave His only begotten Son, that whoever believes in Him should <u>not perish</u> but have <u>everlasting life.</u>*
*NKJV*

If we believe in Jesus, what can we be assured that we will *not* experience?

<u>　hot perish　</u>

If we believe in Jesus, what can we be assured that we *will* experience?

<u>　everlasting life　</u>

3.　　Romans 10:9-13

Underline the phrases "Everyone who calls on the name of the Lord will be saved."

*9 That if you confess with your mouth, "Jesus is Lord," and believe in your heart that God raised him from the dead, you will be saved. 10 For it is with your heart that you believe and are justified, and it is with your mouth that you confess and are saved. 11 As the Scripture says, "Anyone who trusts in him will never be put to shame." 12 For there is no difference between Jew and Gentile-the same Lord is Lord of all and richly blesses all who call on him, 13 for, "<u>Everyone who calls on the name of the Lord will be saved.</u> NIV*

Who can be saved? <u>everyone who calls</u>

What must we believe in our hearts? <u>Jesus is Lord & God raised him from death</u>

What must we say or confess with our mouths? <u>Jesus is Lord</u>

If we believe in our heart that God raised Jesus from the dead and if we confess with our mouth that He is our Lord, what is the result?

_We will be saved_

Do you believe that Jesus was raised from the dead by God? _Yes_

Have you ever made the decision to surrender your life to God and invite Jesus to be the Lord of your life?

_Yes_

**☙Nugget☙** Perhaps you are the type of person that has always believed in God or gone to church. You consider yourself to be a spiritual person and God has been a part of your thinking for many years. Maybe you are the person who has believed that Jesus rose from the dead for years; you celebrate Easter every year. That's great, but it's not enough. If you want to be saved, it requires more than just believing. The Bible says that the devil himself believes and trembles. So, we can see that belief alone is not enough, otherwise the devil himself would be saved and we are certain that he is not saved! Notice what this passage says. Believing in Jesus is only half of the salvation equation. The other half of the equation is a personal confession of faith; it's you saying to God, with your mouth, _"Jesus be the Lord of my life."_ What does that mean? Is that just giving God empty lip service? Is that just parroting a prayer? Not hardly. To confess with your mouth that Jesus is Lord is to make a decision to cross the line of faith by surrendering the lordship of your life to Him. In essence, you humble yourself and give up control of the steering wheel of your life and you invite Him to be the Lord of you. He becomes "the Boss of you"! To confess Jesus as Lord is to verbally acknowledge that He has taken His rightful place as the Lord of your life and you have taken the place of submission to His leadership.

## Are You Ready To Make Your Reservation?

Again, let's ask the question, if you were to die today and stand before God, would you be ready for the judgment? If God were to ask you, *"Why should I let you into heaven?"*, what would you say? Is your name on God's Guest List? Does He have a reservation for you? Have you made your reservation for eternity? We usually plan ahead for important things in life, don't we? We plan for retirement. We plan for our children's college education. We make reservations for dinner, airline tickets and rental cars, but how many of us have really given thought to where we will spend eternity? The apostle John recorded this about God's Guest List: *"And I saw the dead, small and great, stand before God; and the books were opened and another book was opened, which is the book of life (God's Guest List): and the dead were judged out of those things which were written in the books . . . and whosoever was not found written in the book of life (God's Guest List) was cast into the lake of fire." Revelation 20:12, 15*

Perhaps you are on other people's lists. Maybe you're on some type of *Who's Who* list, or the "respected people in your town" list, or "high achievers in your vocation" list, or the "hard workers of America" list . . . or any other esteemed list. That's wonderful, but the big question is this: *"Are you on God's Guest List?"* This is one list you definitely want to be on—God's Guest List for heaven! If your name is not found written on His list, you are in big trouble; trouble that will last for eternity!

Would you like to know how to get your name on God's Guest List? How to make your reservation for eternity? It is actually quite simple. Jesus told us plainly when He said, *"For God so loved the world, that He gave His only begotten Son, that whosoever believeth in Him should not perish, but have everlasting life." John 3:16* He went on to say, *"Verily, verily, I say unto you, He that heareth My word, and believeth on Him that sent Me, hath everlasting life, and shall not come into condemnation; but is passed from death unto life." John 5:24* The key to getting on God's Guest List is believing in Jesus Christ whom He sent. Jesus said, *"I am the way, the truth, and the life: no man cometh unto the Father, but by Me." John 14:6*

Making your reservation for heaven is as simple as humbling yourself, submitting your life to God and inviting Jesus Christ into your life. The moment you acknowledge your need for Jesus and genuinely invite Him to be your Lord, your reservation is made! It is not something to be taken lightly, because God takes you at your word. When you allow Jesus into your heart and when you confess Him as your Lord, He promises that He will take you to heaven forever. Jesus said, *"Whosoever therefore shall confess Me before men, him will I confess also before my Father which is in heaven. But whosoever shall deny Me before men, him will I also deny before My Father which is in heaven." Matthew 10:32, NKJV*

This simple decision is the beginning of eternal life. A new kind of relationship with God begins to blossom within you. This new-found life is just a taste of what you will experience for eternity. You can be certain that your name is in the book of life, God's Guest List. You can be certain that you have a reservation for eternity. You can know where you will spend eternity and you will experience freedom from the fear of death.

Are you ready to surrender to God, ask Him to forgive your sins and invite Jesus Christ to be the Lord of your life?

If so, I encourage you to pray something like:

*Dear God, I am not sure if my name is on Your Guest List, but I want to be sure that it is. I know that Jesus Christ is the way to You and to heaven. I make a decision to humble myself and I submit my life to You, Lord. I do believe that Jesus Christ is Your son and has risen from the dead. Jesus, I invite You into my heart to be the Lord of my life. Thank You, Jesus, for saving me. Thank You that my name is now being written in Your book of life— Your Guest List. Help me to live a life that is pleasing to You until I see You in heaven. In Jesus' Name, Amen.*

What must I do to be saved? The Jailer Acts 16:30

## Scriptures To Chew On

Taking time to meditate on and memorize God's Word is invaluable. Hiding His Word in our hearts will strengthen us for the present and arm us for the future. Here are two verses to memorize and chew on this week. Write these verses on index cards and carry them with you this week. If you will post them in your bathroom, dashboard, desk, locker or other convenient places, you will find these Scriptures taking root in your heart.

*"This is the testimony in essence: God gave us eternal life; the life is in his Son.*
*So, whoever has the Son, has life; whoever rejects the Son, rejects life.*
*My purpose in writing is simply this: that you who believe in God's Son will*
*know beyond the shadow of a doubt that you have eternal life,*
*the reality and not the illusion."*
*1 John 5:11-14, The Message*

*"I tell you the truth,*
*whoever hears my word and believes him who sent me has eternal life*
*and will not be condemned; he has crossed over from death to life."*
*John 5:24, NIV*

## Group Discussion

1.    Describe some of the things you have believed about life after death.

2.    Describe your own experience of living with the fear of death.

3.    Describe your salvation experience, if you've come to Christ.
      What happened? If you'd like to receive Christ, please let someone in
      your Small Group know and allow them to pray the prayer on the
      previous page with you.

---

[1] Rawlings, Maurice. Beyond Death's Door. Nashville; Bantam, 1991.

# Fear Of Man

Have you ever been so "self-conscious" about something that it brought you into fear, panic or an anxiety attack? Fear is paralyzing; that's the point. The enemy wants to use fear to paralyze, stop and hinder us from fulfilling God's will. He wants us so "self-conscious" that we are not God-conscious or Word-conscious. The fear of man makes us conscious of ourselves, rather than aware of being obedient to God. Fear of man keeps us from being a witness for Jesus. We focus on ourselves and wonder, do we look like geeks? Do we sound stupid? Are we cool? Are we going to embarrass ourselves? Will we be laughed at? Ignored? Persecuted? All of these fears can be traced back to the fear of man.

When we operate under the fear of man—what they think of us, say about us, do to us—we live in bondage. They become our lord. The fear of man will keep you in a job you hate, in relationships that are co-dependent and dysfunctional, living so far below your potential it's pitiful and regrettable. It's time to break free from the fear of man and live in the fear of God, where there is freedom and life!

Social phobias keep many people from the joy of relationships. I knew a woman once who told me that she was afraid to go to the mall. I asked her why and she said it was because she did not feel like she had a right to be there. She did not feel worthy of going to the mall. The people there scared her. She literally could not go to the mall and walk through the stores for a fear of people. How sad. Many people suffer from the subtle yet debilitating fear of people and social settings that keeps them in bondage.

> Never take counsel of your fears.
> Andrew Jackson

☙

# How I Learned This Lesson

I've always been a fairly outgoing person, comfortable talking with just about anyone, and have often found myself in leadership positions. Fear of people was never an issue for me, until I faced a season of being stretched in just about every direction and was vulnerable to people's comments. A man in our church made a comment about me that the enemy used to rock my world. One day this man wrote us a note and said, *"Why does she speak? She has nothing to say."* That comment was like a fiery dart that pierced my heart. The devil used those 8 words to attack my life and send me into the bondage of being concerned with the "fear of man." Up until this time, I had been confident to speak in front of groups (which I had done quite a bit), but I was suddenly unusually nervous before speaking and felt intimidated. I found myself afraid to get up in front of a group to share announcements, much less a sermon, for fear of people!

At that same time, I also noticed that when I watched others speak or even as I watched the news anchors on TV, this thought would go through my mind: *"I don't want to speak anymore. I would never want to be on TV. I am so glad I don't do that."* This was such a strange experience for me, because at that time I had no intention of being in the news business and never imagined that I would be on TV, reporting the news or preaching a sermon. A television ministry was not on our radar screen at all, which is why these thoughts troubled me so much. This "fear of man" temptation and satanic attack went on for months. The confidence I once had in the Lord had been replaced by the "fear of man" and I knew I needed to seek the Lord to get back to the place of confidence in God!

I recognized that I was undergoing a spiritual attack and I earnestly sought the Lord for His wisdom and His Word to be set free from this terrible fear of man. I knew His Word would work. God's Word became my medicine! I began to look up every verse I could find regarding freedom from the fear of man, anxiety, worry, and fear in general. I meditated on those verses. I looked up verses of Scripture regarding the Lord as my confidence and I meditated on those verses as well. I sought the Lord!

During that season the Lord showed me two things.

**First**, He reassured me that as I meditated on His Word in this area that through the help of the Holy Spirit He would cause me to be completely set free from the fear of man and He would bring me back to a place of confidence in Him.

**Second**, He showed me that I needed to make a change in my lifestyle in one area of diet. The Lord told me, *"Get off coffee."* Coffee? Yes, coffee. I was a coffee addict. I had been drinking lots of coffee during the previous several years. It was my "Christian drug." Drinking coffee had helped me lose weight after each of my pregnancies, kept me awake and alert to function with the pace of life during various seasons of raising four babies and helping my husband pioneer a church. I was addicted to coffee. I loved the thought, smell and taste of coffee. The only problem was that coffee was controlling me more than I was controlling it. I drank so much coffee that I am convinced I threw my body chemistry off in a big way. I felt like my adrenal glands were constantly in the state of *"fight or flight."* When the Lord told me to, *"Get off coffee,"* I knew what He meant—quit drinking coffee and get free from the addiction. To make a long story short, I finally obeyed the Lord and quit drinking coffee. I immediately felt the benefits in my body. It was like my body said, *"Thank you for taking your foot off the gas pedal. Now I can relax a bit."* A sense of calm and peace filled me internally. Those feelings of anxiety and the fear of man diminished until finally, they just left.

I believe the combination of seeking the Lord, believing His Word and obeying Him in the area of my diet led to freedom from the fear of man in this season of my life.

☙**Nugget**❧ There is an interesting side note, however. Within six months, guess what happened? The Lord led us to begin broadcasting on television a Bible class I teach titled, *"Getting A Grip On The Basics"*. God led us to do the very thing the enemy had tried to thwart through the fear of man. This TV Bible class has been airing in about a dozen local communities, and we're always surprised to hear how many people watch it and we're blessed to hear good reports of how God has used it to encourage people in their walk with God. I find it interesting that the very thing the devil tried to use to keep me in fear—i.e., TV—ended up being the very thing the Lord led us to do. As you know, the enemy often recognizes God's hand in our lives before we do, and he does his best to set traps for us or send trials and fear into our lives to keep us from fulfilling God's will and influencing others for Christ.

☙**Nugget**❧ One more side bar—regarding coffee. I am not against coffee! In my case, the Lord wanted to help me get free from a coffee addiction. Perhaps in your life it's some other addiction, cigarettes, TV, wine or some other thing that controls your life. God wants us to live in moderation under His control. God is intimately acquainted with us, He knows the things that have a grip on us and He knows how to give us a customized strategy for freedom if we will sincerely and earnestly call on Him. In my life, after being "coffee free" for two years, the Lord let me know that the addiction to coffee was broken! I never have any intention of becoming the coffee addict that I once was, but I have found that I can enjoy a cappuccino or latte as long as I keep things in moderation. The point of my story is that God wants to help us through both spiritual and natural means to be free from fear, and in particular the fear of man. In the same way that He had a strategy for me, He has one for you!

Let's take a look at this subject, the fear of man.

## Don't Be Afraid Of The People

1.      Jeremiah 1:4-9

Underline the phrase "don't be afraid of the people."

*4 The LORD gave me a message. He said, 5 "I knew you before I formed you in your mother's womb. Before you were born I set you apart and appointed you as my spokesman to the world." 6 "O Sovereign LORD," I said, "I can't speak for you! I'm too young!" 7 "Don't say that," the LORD replied, "for you must go wherever I send you and say whatever I tell you. 8 And don't be afraid of the people, for I will be with you and take care of you. I, the LORD, have spoken!" 9 Then the LORD touched my mouth and said, "See, I have put my words in your mouth!" NLT*

What did God call Jeremiah to do? _____

What was Jeremiah's fear? _____

Who should we obey—our fears or God? _____

What did the Lord promise? _____

How did the Lord help Jeremiah? _____

2. Psalm 56:4

Underline the words "I will not be afraid."

*In God, whose word I praise, in God I trust; I will not be afraid. What can mortal man do to me? NIV*

What two things did the psalmist do in order to remain free from the fear of man?

_____

_____

If we want to be free from the fear of man or any flesh, it's not just automatic; these two things are critical.

**First,** we have to purposely praise, adhere to, cling to, attend to and believe God's Word. We have to believe that God's Word is more powerful and a higher authority than anyone else's Word—including your own voice of doubts, well meaning loved ones, doctors, bankers, lawyers and every other voice clamoring for your attention. God's voice, as revealed through His Word, becomes the standard for our lives and the highest authority for truth and reality. There is security and stability in

No one loves the man whom he fears.
Aristotle

being anchored in the Word. In order to bank our lives on the Word, we have to know what the Word says, and that requires our discipline to read and meditate on it. As we feed on the Word, it drops down into our hearts and becomes a part of our life.

**Second,** we have to purposely place our trust in God. It's simple in theory, right? We must transfer our trust from anything other than God and by faith lean on His everlasting arms, regardless what people around us think, say or do. Often, we trust in other people instead of God. We trust others to do business in our stores, buy our products, support our ministries and help us succeed in many facets of life. The problem is misplaced trust. Our success is not contingent on people; it's contingent on our obedience to God.

≈**Nugget**≈ As a person in ministry, I understand this temptation. In our roles as pastors, if my husband and I lived in the fear of not offending others, not petting them enough, living up to their expectations, being all things to all men so that everyone liked us, we'd be busy disobeying God. As a result, His church and what He's called us to do would suffer. We'd be slaves to people, not Jesus. Of course, at times it's a real temptation because we all want people to like us and approve of us, but it cannot be at the expense of God's approval.

Think about it in real life: what if you ticked off your biggest customer or the largest giver to your ministry? What if you upset all your employees or volunteers? What if you didn't cater to the whiners and gossips? They'd like you to think they have the power to destroy you, your company, your reputation or your ministry. They don't!

I have a little saying that I remind myself of from time to time. It has served me well in life and ministry, and it's simply this: *"I have Friends in high places."* Yes, I do. My Friends are God my Father, Jesus my Lord and the Holy Spirit my Helper! I believe my friendship with Him trumps all others! God is the One who knows everyone and has all the power and connections. In one millisecond He can do what it would take an army and half the billionaires on the planet to accomplish in my life. I am not looking to those with the most power, money, influence or status to make my life, marriage, family or ministry successful; I am looking to my Friends in High Places. As I follow God He will put me over and fulfill His good pleasure in my life.

3.      Psalm 27:1

Underline the phrase "whom shall I fear."

*The LORD is my light and my salvation; whom shall I fear? The LORD is the strength of my life; of whom shall I be afraid? KJV*

If the Lord is your light, salvation and the strength of your life, whom should you fear?

_____

What do you think it means for the Lord to be your light, salvation and strength?

_____

4.      Psalm 118:6

Underline the phrase "I will not fear."

*The LORD is on my side; I will not fear: what can man do unto me? KJV*

The secret to not being in the fear of man is what? _____

_____

Do you believe and know for certain that God is on your side? He is! Romans 8:31-32 tells us, ". . . *If God is for us, who can be against us? He who did not spare his own Son, but gave him up for us all-how will he not also, along with him, graciously give us all things?" NIV* You and God are a majority! Think about it. No one can stand against you if God is for you, and He is!

5.      Proverbs 29:25

Underline the phrase "trusts in the Lord."

*The fear of man brings a snare, but whoever trusts in the LORD shall be safe. NKJV*

What does the fear of man bring? _____

How would you describe a snare? _____

6.      Hebrews 13:6

Underline the phrase "I will not fear."

*So we may boldly say: "The LORD is my helper; I will not fear. What can man do to me? NKJV*

What is our bold confession? _____

How does knowing that the Lord is your helper eliminate your fear of man?

_____

Again, freedom from the fear of man goes back to heartfelt trust in God.

7.      Matthew 10:26-31

Underline the phrase "don't be afraid."

*26 But don't be afraid of those who threaten you. For the time is coming when everything will be revealed; all that is secret will be made public. 27 What I tell you now in the darkness, shout abroad when daybreak comes. What I whisper in your ears, shout from the housetops for all to hear! 28 "Don't be afraid of those who want to kill you. They can only kill your body; they cannot touch your soul. Fear only God, who can destroy both soul and body in hell. 29 Not even a sparrow, worth only half a penny, can fall to the ground without your Father knowing it. 30 And the very hairs on your head are all numbered. 31 So don't be afraid; you are more valuable to him than a whole flock of sparrows. NLT*

What do these passages tell us not to fear? _____

Who does this passage tell us to fear? _____

Peter knew first hand the bitterness of falling subject to the fear of man. He vowed that he would not deny the Lord but would take a bold stand for Jesus, yet when it came right down to it, he fell victim to the fear of man and denied the Lord three times. Matthew 26:33-35 gives us the details of Peter's faith statement. *"Peter answered and said to Him, "Even if all are made to stumble because of You, I will never be made to stumble." Jesus said to him, "Assuredly, I say to you that this night, before the rooster crows, you will deny Me three times." Peter said to Him, "Even if I have to die with You, I will not deny You!" And so said all the disciples."* NKJV Fortunately, Jesus restored Peter after he denied the Lord, and Peter became one of Jesus' most vocal and fruitful disciples. His godly sorrow worked a repentance that bore much fruit!

8.     Matthew 10:32-33

Underline the words "confess/confesses" and "denies or deny."

*32 Therefore whoever confesses Me before men, him I will also confess before My Father who is in heaven. 33 But whoever denies Me before men, him I will also deny before My Father who is in heaven. NKJV*

He who is afraid of a thing gives it power over him.
Moorish Proverb

If we confess Jesus in front of others, what will He do for us? _____

_____

If we deny Jesus in front of others, what will He do? _____

_____

9.    Mark 8:38

Underline the word "embarrassed."

*If any of you are embarrassed over me and the way I'm leading you when you get around your fickle and unfocused friends, know that you'll be an even greater embarrassment to the Son of Man when he arrives in all the splendor of God, his Father, with an army of the holy angels. The Message*

Jesus warned his followers about getting fickle in our faith around our friends.

If we are embarrassed about Jesus, what did He say we would be?

_____

Describe a time when you were tempted to be embarrassed about your faith in Jesus.

_____

_____

# Be A God Pleaser

God calls us to live a life pleasing to Him, for His approval. When we do that, we experience the joy of the Lord as our strength and the peace which passes all understanding! When we experience the joy and peace that comes from pleasing God, we often wonder why we were even tempted to live under the fear of pleasing man!

1.      Colossians 1:10

        Underline the phrase "please him in every way."

        *And we pray this in order that you may live a life worthy of the Lord and may please him in every way: bearing fruit in every good work, growing in the knowledge of God . . . NIV*

        What type of life does God want us to live? _____

2.      1 Thessalonians 2:4-6

        Underline the phrases "not trying to please men" and "not looking for praise from men."

        *4 On the contrary, we speak as men approved by God to be entrusted with the gospel. We are not trying to please men but God, who tests our hearts. 5 You know we never used flattery, nor did we put on a mask to cover up greed-God is our witness. 6 We were not looking for praise from men, not from you or anyone else. NIV*

        Who are we trying to please? _____

        Whose praise are we seeking? _____

        In what ways do you find this challenging? _____

3.      John 12:42-43

Underline the phrases "praise from men" and "praise from God."

*42 Yet at the same time many even among the leaders believed in him. But because of the Pharisees they would not confess their faith for fear they would be put out of the synagogue; 43 for they loved praise from men more than praise from God. NIV*

Fear of man costs a lot! These leaders lost the privilege of following Jesus because of the fear of man.

Why did these leaders hide their faith? _____

Whose praise did they receive in being silent? _____

Whose praise would they not receive? _____

≈**Nugget**≈ To be a God pleaser rather than a man pleaser doesn't mean that you become a rude ingrate! God calls us to love and serve people, yet we are not to be ensnared by the fear of man. I believe as we trust God and live to please Him alone, He actually gives us favor with man and positions us for His greatest will in our lives. He gets all the glory, we get the blessings and people get helped. It's a great plan!

## One Little Caveat

When we make the decision to live free from the fear of man we still need to walk in love toward people. God wants us to please Him, but we are to love, honor and submit to one another. Walking in the godly balance of being free from the fear of man while at the same time loving, honoring and submitting to man in our marriage, employment, church and daily life is our goal. So, while we don't live in the fear of man or in being a man-pleaser, the Bible does say we are to submit to one another in love.

Unfortunately, there are those in business, education, government, ministry and life that operate with an arrogant, ego-driven, dictatorial, controlling and overbearing spirit, and they expect everyone around them to bow down and submit to their leadership. Because of an overemphasis on submission, many genuine-hearted believers have been duped by these manipulators and held in bondage by submitting to these types of leaders. There are rebel personalities that manipulate the Scriptures and refuse to submit to anyone's authority—whether it's their parents, the government, their boss or their pastor. This is not God's plan.

Our goal is to be a God-pleaser! I love the way a preacher friend of ours says it, *"We live for an audience of One."* As we genuinely submit our lives to the Lord and seek Him, He will show us natural and supernatural strategies to live a life free from the fear of man. He will be our Friend in High Places and He will help us identify, honor and submit to the authorities He has placed in our lives.

## Scriptures To Chew On

Taking time to meditate on and memorize God's Word is invaluable. Hiding His Word in our hearts will strengthen us for the present and arm us for the future. Here are two verses to memorize and chew on this week. Write these verses on index cards and carry them with you this week. If you will post them in your bathroom, dashboard, desk, locker or other convenient places, you will find these Scriptures taking root in your heart.

*"And don't be afraid of the people,*
*for I will be with you and take care of you. I, the LORD, have spoken!"*
*Jeremiah 1:8, NLT*

*"Now the Lord is the Spirit; and where the Spirit of the Lord is, there is liberty."*
*2 Corinthians 3:17-18, NKJV*

## Group Discussion

1.   Describe your experience with the "fear of man."

2.   Describe how you deal with people that try to control, intimidate, manipulate or dictate your life? How do you balance setting up boundaries and living free from the fear of man with loving, honoring and submitting to others?

3.   Describe what being a "God pleaser" or "living for an audience of One" means to you. How do you walk this out?

## Fear Of Danger

Class V white water is beautiful, but treacherous, unpredictable, angry, turbulent, powerful and in your face. *A lot like the times we are living in.* The fifteen-mile stretch of the New River in West Virginia winds through trees and rocks with 25 Class III, IV and V rapids calling your name. We learned that having a good guide and being in the right raft can be a matter of life and death.

## Life Lessons From A Rafting Trip

Our family of six, plus our guide and two strangers jumped into the yellow and blue raft and we slapped, screamed and cut into the fast moving river with an intensity I had never experienced. This wasn't the "Make New Friends Canoe Trip" I remembered from Girl Scouts, it was a life or death event.

After lunch we hit the first and most dangerous Class V rapids. Adrenaline was pumping, the guide was barking out orders and every one of us was screaming, *"Paddle!"* as we made it through the daunting three-part rapids. All of a sudden a whistle blew and when we looked up river, we saw that the raft behind us had flipped over. Our guide had that grave, panicked look on his face. An empty, upside-down raft, sixteen paddles and eight rafters were floating rapidly towards us. We tried to rescue them before they hit big rocks, deadly hydraulic water pulls or entrapment in underwater debris known as the "meat grinder".

We were able to rescue two rafters. They were in shock, as were we. We watched helplessly as the other rafters were pulled downstream by the rapid current and massive volume of treacherous water.

You gain strength, courage and confidence by every experience in which you really stop to look fear in the face. You are able to say to yourself. "I lived through this horror. I can take the next thing that comes along. Eleanor Roosevelt

Downstream we all parked on shore in a calm section of the river to do a head count. Everyone was shaken. Within minutes it became obvious that one rafter was still missing. For the next two hours a search and rescue was conducted by expert rapid water rescue teams. That day there was a tragedy. A fourteen-year-old girl in our group was entrapped and died.

When the unthinkable death was announced, I felt a million emotions at once. My heart broke for her poor father; he was devastated and in shock. At the same time, I desperately wanted to get my family safely off that river. Fear tried to grip us. I prayed. I prayed some more. Every ounce of human courage was drained from my body and mind. I wanted to wake up from this very bad dream and find my family safe and sound on shore.

Unfortunately, there was only way off the river: paddle! With more Class IV and V rapids ahead, my husband and I had to dig as deep as we had ever dug, to trust the Lord for faith and courage to overcome the fear that stared us in the face. The Lord helped us find courage so we could finish. We paddled. We lived.

In looking back on that day, I can't imagine that rafting trip without our guide. The river moves at a rapid rate of speed, there are dangers at every turn. Fortunately, the guide had done the river many times and was well acquainted with every turn and hidden danger in the river. He called out an order, we obeyed. Thankfully, he navigated our family to safety.

That rafting trip was a real life parable for the times we are living in. It's a dangerous world out there. The current of world events is moving at a rapid rate of speed. There are dangers on every hand and evil lurks at every turn. Terrorism. Disease. Nuclear threats. Suicide bombers. Earthquakes. Tsunamis. Crime. Sexual predators. Biological and chemical weapons. I can't imagine life without the help of our experienced Guide. If we'll follow His Word and leadings, He helps navigate us through the dangerous spots on the river of life.

## These Are Dangerous Times

We are definitely living in an age of danger. The Bible tells us just exactly what the last days would look like. See if this doesn't describe our times: *"Don't be naive. There are difficult times ahead. As the end approaches, people are going to be self-absorbed, money-hungry, self-promoting, stuck-up, profane, contemptuous of parents, crude, coarse, dog-eat-dog, unbending, slanderers, impulsively wild, savage, cynical, treacherous, ruthless, bloated windbags, addicted to lust, and allergic to God. They'll make a show of religion, but behind the scenes they're animals. Stay clear of these people."* 2 Timothy 3:1-5, The Message Jesus told us that danger would come. *"The nations and kingdoms will proclaim war against each other, and there will be famines and earthquakes in many parts of the world. But all this will be only the beginning of the horrors to come. 'Then you will be arrested, persecuted, and killed. You will be hated all over the world because of your allegiance to me . . .'"* Matthew 24:7-9, NLT

Since 9/11 there has been a heightened state of alert in our nation, and people are dealing with an entirely new level of fear and anxiety. A few months after 9/11, my husband and I were flying home from Florida. People were on edge and suspicious of everyone on the airplane. You could feel people scoping each other out. I settled into the middle seat, hoping that no one would take the aisle seat as I really wanted to sleep in comfort. At the last moment, a Middle Eastern looking man made his way to the seat next to mine. Immediately, I began to size him up: *"Is he a terrorist? Does he have a bomb strapped to his body? How will I take him down?"* I watched his every move; although my face was looking straight ahead, I stretched my eyeballs to angles they had never been to watch this potential terrorist. I noticed he kept looking at his watch and I thought, *"Ok, he's got a timer on the bomb . . . mmmm, what time did he set it for? Why is he looking so nervous?"* When he reached down to pull up his socks, I was sure the bomb was in his shoe.

Finally, he relaxed and our airplane took off. I relaxed as well, and decided that perhaps he wasn't a terrorist. I fell asleep. When the flight attendant came by later to offer us drinks, I woke up and decided that maybe I ought to be friendly instead of suspicious! I engaged the man in small talk, secretly thinking that if we became friends, maybe he would spare my life! As it turned out, he wasn't from the Middle East, but India. He had been doing contract work in Florida and was flying home to India to see his family, whom he had been separated from for the past 8 months. He told me he missed his family. He said he was afraid to fly and nervous about the very long flight ahead of him. Wow, did I feel terrible. Here I was, mentally practicing my kung fu moves to save the airplane from this terrorist, and he was just a scared guy from India desperately wanting to get home to his wife and children. It was then I decided that rather than giving him the death grip I had planned, perhaps I ought to share Jesus and freedom from fear with him! In time, I began to ask him about his religion—he told me he didn't know which god he believed in. I took this as my cue and talked to him about Jesus, the Prince of peace.

People are anxious about terrorism. Their health. The safety of their children. The economy. It's a dangerous world and whether it's the Asian tsunami and 500 mph waves, unusual hurricanes, freak accidents, massive earthquakes, suitcase nukes, sexual predators or demonically motivated people—it's a scary world out there without Jesus Christ and His promise of wisdom and protection.

Does God want His children living in fear? Panic? Anxiety? Absolutely not! Does the Lord want believers to live like an ostrich burying their heads in the sand pretending evil doesn't exist? No. Does Jesus want us to live in the state of *"Well, you just never know . . ."* No, not when He's given us His Word so that we could know.

God wants us to be realistic about the dangers around us, and yet full of faith, courage, peace and love. God has given us His Word and wisdom for living a life free from the fear of danger.

&**Nugget**&  There are some fundamental things we need to understand if we want to live a life free from the fear of danger. We need to know where God stands on this. Is He sending evil, tragedy, calamity, terror, disease or scary times to get our attention? Teach us? Humble us? Or, is another force behind the danger around us? Let's look at this subject.

# We Live In A Fallen World

We live in a fallen world. What does that mean? Let's take a moment to do a quick study on this and see if we can glean some helpful truths that will give us wisdom and set us free from the fear of danger.

According to God's Word, when Adam and Eve were created God gave them dominion and authority over all the earth. When they sinned in the garden the whole world fell under the curse of the fall as Adam delivered the authority of the kingdoms of the world to the devil. The result was that satan, the devil, became the god of this fallen world. His mission is to wreak havoc on God's creation by stealing, killing and destroying wherever he can. His method is to keep people in bondage to fear, weakness and an undisciplined mind. *(Genesis 1:26-28, Psalm 8:5-6, Psalm 115:16, Genesis 3, Luke 4:5, 2 Corinthians 4:4, 2 Timothy 1:7, John 10:10)* The devil initiates evil and He wants us to live in the fear of danger.

God wants us to live free from the fear of danger and in order to start the process, we must understand a fundamental truth: God does not *cause* evil, tragedy, horror, disease or calamity. He knows it happens and sometimes He has to *permit* these things, but He is not *initiating* them. This is a huge truth that we must grasp! Let's look at a few reasons God must permit evil.

One reason bad things happen is simply because we live in a fallen world where because satan operates as the god of this world. He initiates and motivates people to do all kinds of bad things. Another reason bad things happen is because people have a free will and often they yield to their fleshly desires. God allows people to be evil or fleshly if they so choose. Sometimes bad things happen because we disobey God's Word and judgment comes. In all of these situations, God must *permit* danger, evil, tragedy, terror, calamity and bad things to happen, but He is not *initiating* them.

You can discover what your enemy fears most by observing the means he uses to frighten you.
Eric Hoffer

Bad things also happen because sometimes people break spiritual and physical laws. For example, if we break the law of gravity by jumping off the Golden Gate Bridge, we'll plunge to our demise. God has set up spiritual laws that operate in the same way, and if we break these laws there is a good chance that danger, tragedy, calamity, trouble and danger will result. For example, God's law of sowing and reaping is a wonderful law! However, if we sow bad seeds into our bodies by smoking our entire life, there is a good chance that we may reap lung cancer or emphysema. God does not send the lung cancer or the emphysema, but He has to permit it as the harvest of the seed we have sown. Make sense?

This is an important truth, because if we somehow think that God is the author of the terrible things around us, then how can we ever get free from fear and trust Him to protect and guide us? If we believe God sends evil, sickness, terror, criminals, freak accidents, devastating weather and other calamities to teach us a lesson, to humble us, correct us or to get our attention then how can we believe that He cares for us and find freedom from the fear of danger? God is not schizophrenic—He's not good one day and bad the next. He's good all the time. He's a good Father and He does not abuse His kids. What would you call a parent that inflicts their child with the threat of danger, evil, tragedy, calamity, sickness or terror? We call those parents abusive! Why do we think God would send those things to us? He's a good father isn't He? He's not "moody" and shifting like the shadows. He's a good God who gifts good gifts—all the time. *(Matthew 7:11, James 1:17)*

Let's look at another example. Think about weather and Jesus' ministry. He rebuked a few storms during his life and ministry. Were the storms that Jesus rebuked "acts of God" as some people today believe? If God were the author of storms, tornadoes and hurricanes, then did Jesus rebuke God when He rebuked the storms and wind? Of course not! Jesus rebuked dangerous weather that had been stirred up because we live in a fallen world.

☙**Nugget**☙ Why are people so confused about this? Why do we attribute so many evil things to God? Jesus revealed God's character to us, but unfortunately, because of confusion on a few verses in the Old Testament, people have come up with entire doctrines that are incongruent with God's very nature. By reading a few Scriptures in the Old Covenant that say things like *"the Lord smote . . ."* or *"an evil* *spirit from God . . ."* or *"the Lord hath afflicted her . . ."* we would conclude that God caused evil or bad things to happen to these people, yet according to Dr. Robert Young, a renowned Greek and Hebrew Bible scholar, the verb was written in the permissive tense in the original language rather than the causative tense.[1] According to Adam Clarke's Commentary, the Hebrew language has no mood to express words in the permissive tense.[2] Verses in the Old Testament were translated in the causative tense, rather than in their original permissive tense. This gives the idea that God *causes* evil, disease, tragedy, danger and death, rather than the idea that He has to *permit* these things.

As an example, it says in Exodus 12:23, *"For the LORD will pass through to strike the Egyptians; and when He sees the blood on the lintel and on the two doorposts, the LORD will pass over the door and not allow the destroyer to come into your houses to strike you."* NKJV At first glance it sounds like the Lord strikes people! But as we read further, we actually see that is was *"the destroyer"* who did the striking. Of course, we know the destroyer is the devil. God had to permit the destroyer to bring judgment and kill the people because of their disobedience and stiff neck.

The truth is that God has to permit evil, destruction, disease and calamity when we choose to walk outside the realm of His Word and the spiritual laws He has established.

## God Is Good All The Time

What other evidence do we have to confirm that God is not bringing evil, danger, calamity, sickness, disease, terror and tragedy to our lives? We know because Jesus told us so. Jesus said, *". . . don't you even yet know who I am, even after all the time I have been with you? Anyone who has seen me has seen the Father! So why are you asking to see him? Don't you believe that I am in the Father and the Father is in me? The words I say are not my own, but my Father who lives in me does his work through me. Just believe that I am in the Father and the Father is in me. Or at least believe because of what you have seen me do. 'The truth is, anyone who believes in me will do the same works I have done, and even greater works, because I am going to be with the Father. You can ask for anything in my name, and I will do it, because the work of the Son brings glory to the Father. Yes, ask anything in my name, and I will do it!'" John 14:9-14, NLT* Jesus said if we have seen Him we have seen the Father. We are told in Colossians 1:14-15 that Jesus is the visible image of the invisible God. Jesus revealed the Father to mankind.

❧**Nugget**❧   Did Jesus ever cause evil? Tragedy? Calamity? Did He ever initiate danger or terror? Absolutely not, never once. In fact, He did just the opposite—when storms came, He rebuked them. When sickness and disease brought pain and suffering, Jesus healed all who came to Him. When evil spirits tormented and oppressed people, Jesus cast them out. Everywhere Jesus went He brought healing, protection, peace and life. Acts 10:38 summarizes Jesus mission, *". . . how God anointed Jesus of Nazareth with the Holy Spirit and with power, who went about doing good and healing all who were oppressed by the devil, for God was with Him." NKJV* In fact, you cannot find one verse in the Bible that tells us that God *initiated* evil against anyone that walked in His Word. There is not one account in Jesus' life and ministry where He *initiated* evil, tragedy or danger in the lives of any person. Certainly God corrects us and chastens us—like a good Father He does this with His Word. Jesus told us that He prunes, chastens and cleanses through His Word, not by sending bad things.

Can you see that? We understand that we live in a dangerous world, and while God must permit bad things to happen, He does not cause them. God seeks to find some redemptive value when bad things happen and He is right there to reach people with the gospel, provide comfort, healing, encouragement, miracles, restoration, protection, life, faith, courage, peace and love instead of fear. For those who will believe His Word and follow Him, He offers wisdom, protection from danger and freedom from fear.

Let's look at a few verses of Scripture that remind us that we are in a fallen world where the enemy seeks to steal, kill and destroy.

1.      John 10:10

        Underline the phrase "The thief comes" and "I have come."

*The thief comes only to steal and kill and destroy; I have come that they may have life, and have it to the full. NIV*

Why did Satan come and what is he responsible for? _____

Why did Jesus come? _____

2.     2 Corinthians 4:4-5

Underline what Satan does to unbelievers.

*The god of this age has blinded the minds of unbelievers, so that they cannot see the light of the gospel of the glory of Christ, who is the image of God. NIV*

What is satan called in this passage? _____

I like how the New Living Testament paraphrases this verse:

*" . . . Satan, the god of this evil world . . . " NLT*

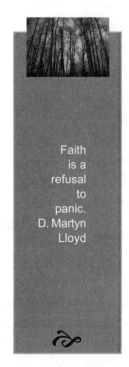

Notice what Ephesians 6:12 calls the devil
and his demons.

*" . . . the rulers of the darkness of this world . . . "*

Faith
is a
refusal
to
panic.
D. Martyn
Lloyd

Ephesians 6:12 reminds us that satan is at work in
the hearts of those who refuse to obey God.

*"You used to live just like the rest of the world,
full of sin, obeying Satan, the mighty prince of
the power of the air. He is the spirit at work in
the hearts of those who refuse to obey God." NLT*

Can you see that, satan is the god of this world
and seeks to influence and fill this world with evil

and darkness?

_____

3.     1 Peter 5:8-9

Underline the phrase "looking for someone to devour."

*8 Be self-controlled and alert. Your enemy the devil prowls around like a roaring lion looking for someone to devour. 9 Resist him, standing firm in the faith. . . NIV*

What is the devil called? _____

What does he seek to do? _____

What are we to do? _____

4.     Luke 10:19

Underline the words "authority" and "power."

*I have given you authority to trample on snakes and scorpions and to overcome all the power of the enemy; nothing will harm you. NIV*

Jesus sent his disciples out with the authority of His Name to preach the gospel and minister to people. When they returned they were filled with joy as they saw first hand the power and authority of Jesus' Name.

What did Jesus give to believers? _____

What can hurt us? _____

᭞**Nugget**᭞ Although we won't go into it in detail, it's important for the believer to understand what the Bible teaches about the authority of the believer in Jesus' Name. Jesus defeated the devil in grand style and He has delegated the use of His Name to the Church and believers today so that we enforce satan's defeat. He's given us the "power of attorney" to use His Name when we face danger. When we receive and believe in Jesus as our Lord, we are transferred from the kingdom of darkness into the kingdom of God's dear Son, and we are given authority in His Name to preach the gospel, faith to move mountains, the ability to overcome the devil and live as more than conquerors through Christ. *(Colossians 1:13, Matthew 28:18-20, Mark 16:15-20, Mark 11:23, Revelation 12:11, Romans 8:37)*

While it's true we live in a fallen world where evil, danger and calamity lurk, as we walk with God, as we grow in the knowledge of God and as we cooperate with His spiritual laws and exercise our authority as believers, we can expect to live free from the fear of danger.

## One Danger We Cannot Escape

Before we look at *Eight Promises Of Protection From Danger* from God's Word, one other thought to consider is this: while we have established the fact that God does not *cause* or *send* danger, evil, tragedy, calamity or terror, there is one danger we cannot escape! Persecution!

Yes, Jesus has promised us that because of our alliance with Him, we will face persecution. We will be hated. We will be treated unfairly. Others will say all kinds of things about us falsely. We may be physically, mentally or emotionally beat up or even killed by those who oppose Jesus and the gospel. God promises to be with us, but persecution will come. He doesn't send it to us, but He will not cause it to cease, either. God never promised to deliver us from persecution. In some cultures, people are killed and martyred for their faith. In other cultures, believers are mocked, laughed at, dissed and dismissed. Jesus told us to not to fear those who can kill our body, but rather to bless those who persecute us and to rejoice and be glad; they persecuted Him, they will persecute us and the result is a great reward in heaven! Now, let's look at the promises of God for protection from danger. *(Matthew 5:11, 44; Luke 11:49, 21:12; John 15:20, Romans 12:14)*

# Eight Promises Of Protection From Danger

When it comes to being free from the fear of danger, what do we know? What has God said concerning His willingness to protect us from evil and danger? Often, in God's Word we see that God's promises are associated with a condition. For example: The promise, " . . . *all things are possible . . .* " has a condition " . . . *to those who believe . . .*" The promise, " . . . *no harm will befall you, no disaster will come near your tent . . .*" has the condition *"If you make the Most High your dwelling . . .* " The promise, *"For God so loved the world . . . you can have everlasting life . . .* " has the condition *"whosoever believes in Him."* Can you see how in many verses of Scripture we have emphasized the promise, without really paying attention to the conditions? There are other verses that simply tell us about God's will and His promise, and the only condition is to believe it! For example, He promises *"to give His angels charge over us to keep us in all our ways."* The only condition is to believe Him! God's Word is loaded with His promises and it's our job to identify those promises, believe Him and fulfill any corresponding conditions.

We can trust God. We can believe His Word. He's not a liar. *"God is not a man, that he should lie, nor a son of man, that he should change his mind. Does he speak and then not act? Does he promise and not fulfill?" Numbers 23:19, NIV* As we look at these verses of Scripture, let's be reminded that God is for us and He has promised us His protection.

Let's begin with Psalm 91, the classic "Protection Psalm," and other Scriptures that can renew our minds.

---

1.      Psalm 91:1-15

        Underline all of God's promises for protection.

        *1 He who dwells in the secret place of the Most High Shall abide under the shadow of the Almighty. 2 I will say of the LORD, "He is my refuge and my fortress; My God, in Him I will trust." 3 Surely He shall deliver you from the snare of the fowler And from the perilous pestilence. 4 He shall cover you with His feathers, And under His wings you shall take refuge; His truth shall be your shield and buckler. 5 You shall not be afraid of the terror by night, Nor of the arrow that flies by day, 6 Nor of the pestilence that walks in darkness, Nor of the destruction that lays waste at noonday. 7 A thousand may fall at your side, And ten thousand at your right hand; But it shall not come near you. 8 Only with your eyes shall you look, And see the reward of the wicked. 9 Because you have made the LORD, who is my refuge, Even the Most High, your dwelling place, 10 No evil shall befall you, Nor shall any plague come near your dwelling; 11 For He shall give His angels charge over you, To keep you in all your ways. 12 In their hands they shall bear you up, Lest you dash your foot against a stone. 13 You shall tread upon the lion and the cobra, The young lion and the serpent you shall trample underfoot. 14 "Because he has set his love upon Me, therefore I will deliver him; I will set him on high, because he has known My name. 15 He shall call upon Me, and I will answer him; I will be with him in trouble; I will deliver him and honor him. 16 With long life I will satisfy him, And show him My salvation. NKJV*

What does God say He will protect us from?
List everything you see in this passage.

_____

_____

_____

Fear is that little darkroom where negatives are developed.
Michael Pritchard

How do you understand verse 7?

_____

What does verse 10 say about God's promise to protect us?

_____

&#x223d;**Nugget**&#x223d; Everyone loves Psalm 91. It's a great passage on God's protection. Perhaps you have a story of God's divine protection in your life. Maybe you are on the other end of the spectrum and have felt as though God did not protect you or your family. Perhaps you're left with lots of "Why God?" questions. As we've already discussed, we live in a fallen world, people have a free will and at times we violate spiritual laws and suffer the consequences. We don't always understand everything that happens, but we know that God is good all the time. We know He is not a liar. We know that Psalm 91 is true and there are times we have to believe that, in spite of our experience, and trust the Lord to explain things to us as we need to know them. Sometimes, we don't have answers, we just have to trust God and know that His Word is true.

Let's look at Psalm 91 more closely and identify the conditions associated with God's promise of protection.

The qualifications or conditions for God's protection according to Psalm 91 are found in verses 1, 2, 4, 9, 14 and 15. What are those conditions?

_____

_____

_____

How do you "dwell in the secret place of the Most High" and "take refuge under His wings"?

_____

_____

&#x223d;**Nugget**&#x223d; What is the secret place? It's a place of peace, protection, love, joy, faith, goodness, grace, victory, comfort, triumph and strength. Everything that God's Presence gives us is found in the secret place of His Presence! One way to stay in the secret place is by spending time in fellowship with God. Talk to Him, read His Word and let Him talk to you. When we love God and love others as ourselves, we are staying in that secret place. When we live our lives in a way that is pleasing to the Lord, by faith we are dwelling in the secret place. When we live by faith, appropriate the Blood and Name of Jesus, and charge our angels to encamp around us, we are living in the secret place.

When you reflect on your life, perhaps you see times that God in His mercy protected you from evil and danger even when you were not abiding by His Word, not living in the secret place and not meeting His conditions. I believe sometimes, when we are non-believers, baby Christians, or ignorant and carnal, God blesses us and protects us simply because He is loving, kind and merciful. Does that make sense? It's because of His mercy that we are not consumed! He's good and it's His will to bless His people; at the same time it's His will that we grow up and walk in obedience to His Word so that His goodness can rest on our lives.

2.      Proverbs 3:25-26

Underline the phrases "be not afraid" and "be thy confidence."

*25 Be not afraid of sudden fear, neither of the desolation of the wicked, when it cometh. 26 For the LORD shall be thy confidence, and shall keep thy foot from being taken. KJV*

What is the promise? _____

What is the condition? _____

3.      Proverbs 18:10

Underline what happens to believers when they run to the name of the Lord.

*The name of the LORD is a strong tower; the righteous run to it and are safe. NKJV*

What is the promise? _____

What is the condition? _____

4.      Proverbs 1:33

Underline the result of hearkening to God's Word.

*But whoso hearkeneth unto me shall dwell safely, and shall be quiet from fear of evil. KJV*

What is the promise? _____

What is the condition? _____

5.      Isaiah 54:13-14

Underline all the things that will be removed from us as we are established in God's Word and righteousness.

*13 All your sons will be taught by the LORD, and great will be your children's peace. 14 In righteousness you will be established: tyranny will be far from you; you will have nothing to fear. Terror will be far removed; it will not come near you. NIV*

What is the promise? _____

What is the condition? _____

6.      Psalm 46:1

Underline God's promise.

*God is our refuge and strength, a very present help in trouble. NKJV*

What does God promise in times of trouble? _____

What does a "very present help" mean to you? _____

_____

7.      Philippians 1:28

Underline all the things the Lord tells us not to do.

*And do not [for a moment] be frightened or intimidated in anything by your opponents and adversaries, for such [constancy and fearlessness] will be a clear sign (proof and seal) to them of [their impending] destruction, but [a sure token and evidence] of your deliverance and salvation, and that from God. AMP*

How long are we to be frightened, intimidated or in fear? _____

What kind of sign is our lack of fear? _____

_____

Do you want to ruin satan's day? Be a fearless Christian, fully trusting in God, and let that remind him of his impending doom.

8.      2 Timothy 1:7

Underline the phrase "a spirit of fear."

*For God has not given us a spirit of fear, but of power and of love and of a sound mind. NKJV*

What does God not give us? _____

What has God given us? _____

_____

## Scriptures To Chew On

Taking time to meditate on and memorize God's Word is invaluable. Hiding His Word in our hearts will strengthen us for the present and arm us for the future. Here are two verses to memorize and chew on this week. Write these verses on index cards and carry them with you this week. If you will post them in your bathroom, dashboard, desk, locker or other convenient places, you will find these Scriptures taking root in your heart.

> *"No evil shall befall you,*
> *Nor shall any plague come near your dwelling;*
> *For He shall give His angels charge over you,*
> *To keep you in all your ways."*
> *Psalm 91:10-11, NKJV*
> *"And I have given you authority over all the power of the enemy,*
> *and you can walk among snakes and scorpions and crush them.*
> *Nothing will injure you."*
> *Luke 10:19, NLT*

## Group Discussion

1. Describe your understanding of living in a fallen world.

2. Describe the idea that God permits danger, but He does not cause it.

3. Which 3 promises of God's protection minister to you the most?

---

[1]Young, Robert. Analytical Concordance to the Bible. Nashville, TN: Thomas Nelson, 1982

[2]Adam Clarke's Commentary, Electronic Database. Copyright © 1996, 2003 by Biblesoft, Inc. All rights reserved.

# Fear Of Change

There is only one thing that doesn't change in this life: God! *"For I am the Lord, I do not change . . ."* Malachi 3:6, NKJV Everything else is subject to change. You. Me. The economy. Our bodies. Our job. Our house. Our children. Technology. If your computer, cell phone, PDA or TV is more than one year old, it's outdated! Things are changing rapidly. You name it and it can change. Some people love change and others hate it; it just depends on your perspective.

In the book *Who Moved My Cheese?,* author Spencer Johnson shares a simple parable that reveals profound truths about change.[1] It's an amusing and enlightening story of four characters that live in a "Maze" and look for "Cheese" to nourish them and make them happy. Things change. They always have changed and always will change. Some of the characters learn how to deal with change and some do not. It's a great little book on the reality of change.

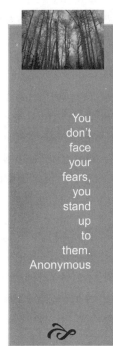

Things are changing rapidly in the business world, and not only do individuals need help overcoming their fear of change, but entire organizations, corporations and even churches need help dealing with the fear of change. I contacted a friend of mine, Dr. Jennifer Palthe, professor of Managing Change at Western Michigan University and former Senior Change Management Consultant with Andersen Consulting, to ask for her expert analysis on the dynamics associated with the fear of change. She said, *"Generally people fear change if they feel threatened by the loss of things of value to them, including their freedom, control, reputation and comfort, due to uncertainty about the unknown (one of the main inducers of stress in the workplace); due to confusion*

You don't face your fears, you stand up to them.
Anonymous

*about what and why things are changing and if change in the past was unsuccessful."*

Dr. Palthe states the importance of appropriately diagnosing the need for change and root causes of fear. *"Like medical doctors misdiagnosing patients with certain illnesses and sometimes generating more harm and genuine fear, so too can organizations misdiagnose the real reasons why change is necessary and thereby induce serious problems that generate confusion and fear. In other words, there may be a genuine willingness on the part of employees to change but if the change has unintended negative consequences (e.g. significant job losses for employees), fear of future change initiatives or new roles may be generated; they may unnecessarily fear change."*

She went on to say, *"To me, fear entertained is change constrained! So, in a world where things are changing so rapidly we all need to be more effective managers of change—people who foresee change and plan accordingly (both personally and professionally). So many change interventions in organizations have failed due to fear and the killer phrases like 'if it ain't broke don't try fix it' or 'be realistic.' Fear feeds off fear, so failed change is a potential precursor to future failures! It's therefore critical that people get over their fears."*

The problem is that most people do not like change. Sure, there are a few adventurous ones who love change (I am one of those people!), but most people don't enjoy it. They like the consistency, stability and security of things not changing. The fear of change locks people into relationships they don't like, jobs they don't like, houses they don't like, cities they don't like, churches they don't like and schools they don't like. You name it! People are trapped because of a fear of change. The fear of change has people locked into patterns of failure and boredom. The fear of change has entire generations of people left behind in this age of technology. In order to succeed in this world you are probably going to need computer and Internet skills. If you are afraid to change because your legal pad and the newspaper are all you need, you will be left behind to enjoy your "horse and wagon" mentality. Don't let the fear of change keep you locked in the dark ages; God has a bright future for you, but it's going to require that you change!

❧**Nugget**❧ When you really think about it, the fear of change is usually associated with the fear of failure, the fear of success or the fear of missing God's will. People are safe and "successful" by their own definitions if they stay the way they are. They know what to expect. They know where they fit in the "pecking order." They know their routines. Change is scary. Unfortunately, as one preacher has said, "If you keep doing what you've always done you will have what you've always had." If you want life to be different for you, it's going to require change!

If you are single and ready to get married, the fear of a failure or missing God's will in marriage may be strong enough to lock you into the fear of change and you'll never pop the question; thus you'll stay safe in your lonely, single life! The fear of failure is seen in the person who won't take the risk to change careers, leave a job they hate and follow the passion God has put in their heart. What if they fail? The fear of change imprisons them, so they'll stay in the job they hate and live an unfulfilled, miserable life. Is that what you want? I doubt it.

Let's get a little closer to home . . . people are trapped in personalities they don't like. They can suffer from anger issues, depression issues, rejection issues, stress issues, weight issues, emotional issues, health issues or job issues because they fear change and fear taking the steps that would improve their lives. There are numerous reasons why; some are valid and based on past experiences and some are not. All of the reasons we fear change can be overcome if we are confident of the Lordship of Jesus Christ in our lives. In order to enjoy the adventure of the Christian life, you and I are going to have to change! We are going to have to live by faith and trust God. It's an exciting way to live life, trusting in God and spitting in the face of the fear of change! Let's look at this subject.

## The One Thing That Doesn't Change

God doesn't change, but everything else does!

1.      Malachi 3:6

   *For I am the LORD, I do not change . . . NKJV*

Who does not change? _____

2.      2 Corinthians 4:18

Underline the words "temporary" and "eternal."

*So we fix our eyes not on what is seen, but on what is unseen. For what is seen is temporary, but what is unseen is eternal. NIV*

If what is seen is temporary, what does that mean? _____

It will change!

## Change Is Safe When You Follow The Lord

Since change is inevitable, let's talk about how to flow with the Lord to enjoy it! The Bible is full of exhortations to change—that is, repent—which means to turn 180 degrees; to change one's mind. If you're going north and you repent, you'll be heading south; you changed!

When we know that we are led by the Spirit into change, there is a certain degree of safety and comfort, even in the midst of having our comfort zone ruffled. I love the way The Message Bible paraphrases Romans 8:14: *"God's Spirit beckons. There are things to do and places to go!"* I hope you find the rest and the energy that comes from following the Lord's leadership. When He is leading us into change, it can be both exciting and safe, as we know He will never lead us astray.

1.      Matthew 4:17

Underline the word "repent."

*From that time Jesus began to preach, and to say, Repent: for the kingdom of heaven is at hand. KJV*

If we want to experience the benefits of God's kingdom, what will we need to do?

_____

2.     1 Thessalonians 1:8-9

Underline the words that describe the change that had happened in these believers' lives.

_8 The word has gotten around. Your lives are echoing the Master's Word, not only in the provinces but all over the place. The news of your faith in God is out. We don't even have to say anything anymore — you're the message! 9 People come up and tell us how you received us with open arms, how you deserted the dead idols of your old life so you could embrace and serve God, the true God. The Message_

These people had a reputation for change.

How would you describe the change that occurred?

_____

How has your life changed since you came to Christ?

_____

_____

_____

_____

_____

Little men with little minds and little imaginations go through life in little ruts, smugly resisting all changes which would jar their little worlds.
Unknown

3.      John 15:1-6

Underline any words that describe change that God initiates.

*1 I am the true vine, and my Father is the gardener. 2 He cuts off every branch that doesn't produce fruit, and he prunes the branches that do bear fruit so they will produce even more. 3 You have already been pruned for greater fruitfulness by the message I have given you. 4 Remain in me, and I will remain in you. For a branch cannot produce fruit if it is severed from the vine, and you cannot be fruitful apart from me. 5 "Yes, I am the vine; you are the branches. Those who remain in me, and I in them, will produce much fruit. For apart from me you can do nothing. NLT*

What type of change does the Lord want in our lives? _____

_____

4.      Proverbs 24:21-22

Underline the word "change."

*21 My son, fear the LORD and the king; do not associate with those given to change; 22 For their calamity will rise suddenly, and who knows the ruin those two can bring? NKJV*

Some people are distracted, unfocused, undisciplined, rebellious and irresponsible; they are always changing their minds, jobs, lovers and friends. This is not the type of change we are talking about. God is not endorsing that type of change.

What is the result of those given to change based on rebellion?

_____

What should our relationship with these types of people be? _____

_____

# By Faith You Can Change

If you've felt stuck in the "same old, same old," life can change for you! Through the power of God's Word you can edit your life. You can reinvent yourself. You can do over. You can succeed at change! It's going to require you to agree with God. You will have to think differently, and this is going to take some effort on your part, but the result will be a transformed you.

It takes faith to change! Unbelief will keep you in the same old, same old. Fear will paralyze you. It's easy to stay the same, but it requires a step of faith and trust in God to make the changes He leads us to. He can be trusted. He has your best interests in mind.

1.      Psalm 56:3

        Underline the phrase "I will trust in You."

        *Whenever I am afraid, I will trust in You. NKJV*

        Anytime you are afraid, what will you choose to do? _____

2.      Proverbs 3:5-6

        Underline the word "trust."

        *5 Trust in the LORD with all your heart, and lean not on your own understanding; 6 In all your ways acknowledge Him, and He shall direct your paths. NKJV*

        How are we to trust the Lord? _____

        What are we not to lean on? _____

        What does God promise? _____

3.      Hebrews 11:6

Underline the thing that pleases God.

*It's impossible to please God apart from faith. And why? Because anyone who wants to approach God must believe both that he exists and that he cares enough to respond to those who seek him. The Message*

If we want to live a life pleasing to the Lord, what must we have? _____

_____

4.      Hebrews 10:38

Circle the lifestyle that pleases the Lord.

*But my righteous one will live by faith. And if he shrinks back, I will not be pleased with him. NIV*

How do believers live? _____

You can do it! Trust God! You can live the adventure-filled life that involves change, by faith.

☙**Nugget**☙ Faith is taking God at His Word. To live by faith means to believe God's Word and to speak God's Word. If He says something in His Word, we choose to believe it, even if we don't feel like it; even if our current circumstances look contrary to it; even if we are afraid—we believe God! When we believe God, we speak His Word, too. By faith, we get our heart and mouth in agreement with God and His Word. For example, if God says "I can do all things through Christ who strengthens me," then by faith in my heart I agree and believe it's true and I begin to say it with my mouth. That's faith! As we hold fast to our confession of faith, God performs His Word, just like He promised. Make sense?

# You Can Be Changed

Are there areas of your life you'd like to change? It's God's desire that we are continually changed and conformed into the image of His Son, Jesus Christ. In order for that happen we are going to have to change— a lot!

1.　　Romans 12:2

In this passage, underline the two phrases that tell us what not to be and what to be.

*And do not be conformed to this world, but be transformed by the renewing of your mind, that you may prove what is that good and acceptable and perfect will of God. NKJV*

Do not be conformed, be transformed!

How would you describe being "transformed"? _____

_____

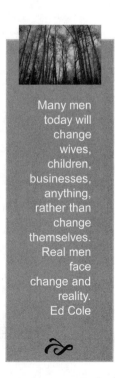

Many men today will change wives, children, businesses, anything, rather than change themselves. Real men face change and reality.
Ed Cole

**Transformed:** The Greek word for this is: "metamorphoo." It means to transform (literally or figuratively, "metamorphose"). It's also translated as change, transfigure, transform.[2]

☞**Nugget**☞ Did you study caterpillars and butterflies in grade school? You know the process of metamorphosis, right? A caterpillar spins a cocoon and the chrysalis is formed to facilitate transformation of this caterpillar into a butterfly! It's amazing. Now, let me ask you a question: have you ever confused a caterpillar with a butterfly? No! Why? Because the process of transformation was so dramatic that the butterfly does not look anything like a caterpillar! The same thing is true when God's transforming power, His supernatural metamorphosis, goes to work in your life. You will be *changed* to such a degree that the new will not look anything at all like the old you!

How are we transformed?

_____

_____

How would you define "renewing of the mind"?

_____

_____

**Renewing of your mind:** Literally, this means the "renovation" of your mind![3]

God wants you to renovate your mind to His Word! He wants you to do a major "fixer upper" job on your thinking by replacing the old, negative, rejected thoughts with the new, true, accepted thoughts His Word is loaded with!

Have you ever been involved in a home renovation project? Describe it:

_____

It takes work to renovate! If you want to be changed into the person God wants you to be, it's going to take work! You'll have to renovate your mind with God's Word.

Are you ready to work on the renovation of your mind? _____

☜**Nugget**☞ You need to get this! The primary way we experience transformation in any area of our lives is by renovating, reprogramming and renewing our minds with God's Word! It's that simple and it's that powerful. Begin to install new thoughts from God's Word into your mind regarding who you are in Christ and you will see the old "caterpillar" you transformed into a new, "butterfly" you! As you meditate on God's Word, how He sees you and who He says you are, the Holy Spirit will bring to your conscious mind the old lies and thoughts you may not even have known you operated by. As these lies are exposed, God can truly do an internal work and real change can begin inside of you. Through trusting God's Word and following the leading of the Holy Spirit, He will work within you the desire and the ability to change and be the person He has called you to be.

2.      1 Samuel 10:6-11

In this passage, underline every word or phrase that describes a change or transformation.

*The Spirit of the LORD will come upon you in power, and you will prophesy with them; and you will be changed into a different person. Once these signs are fulfilled, do whatever your hand finds to do, for God is with you. "Go down ahead of me to Gilgal. I will surely come down to you to sacrifice burnt offerings and fellowship offerings, but you must wait seven days until I come to you and tell you what you are to do." As Saul turned to leave Samuel, God changed Saul's heart, and all these signs were fulfilled that day. When they arrived at Gibeah, a procession of prophets met him; the Spirit of God came upon him in power, and he joined in their prophesying. When all those who had formerly known him saw him prophesying with the prophets, they asked each other, "What is this that has happened to the son of Kish? Is Saul also among the prophets?" NIV*

What happened to Saul? _____

_____

What was it that changed Saul? _____

What did Saul's old friends say? _____

ॐ**Nugget**ॐ God can change you! We see the power of God
changing Saul into a different person! Notice it was God's Spirit coming
upon Saul that changed him. We might say it this way today: when you
allow God's Presence through His Spirit and His Word to saturate your
life, you will be changed!

When the people that formerly knew Saul saw him, they couldn't believe
it! They wanted to know what had happened! This can be true of you,
too! God will change you to such a degree that your old friends will
scratch their heads and try to figure you out!

3.      2 Corinthians 3:18

In this passage, underline the word transfigured. Circle any words or
phrases that describe how this transfiguring happens.

*And all of us, as with unveiled face, [because we] continued to behold*
*[in the Word of God] as in a mirror the glory of the Lord, are constantly*
*being transfigured into His very own image in ever increasing splendor*
*and from one degree of glory to another; [for this comes] from the Lord*
*[Who is] the Spirit. AMP*

If we continue to spend time renovating our minds to God's Word, the
mirror, what will happen to us?

_____

_____

What will we be transfigured or transformed into? _____

_____

The good news is that you don't have to stay the way you are! God has shown us
how to be transformed! We can experience a supernatural metamorphosis
through the power of God's Word! I trust that as you've studied God's Word you

are ready to welcome and embrace change and let the fear of change go! Right? Let the renovation project begin!

## Scriptures To Chew On

Taking time to meditate on and memorize God's Word is invaluable. Hiding His Word in our hearts will strengthen us for the present and arm us for the future. Here are two verses to memorize and chew on this week. Write these verses on index cards and carry them with you this week. If you will post them in your bathroom, dashboard, desk, locker or other convenient places, you will find these Scriptures taking root in your heart.

> *"And do not be conformed to this world,*
> *but be transformed by the renewing of your mind,*
> *that you may prove what is that good and acceptable and perfect*
> *will of God."*
> *Romans 12:2, NKJV*

> *"Trust in the LORD with all your heart,*
> *And lean not on your own understanding;*
> *In all your ways acknowledge Him,*
> *And He shall direct your paths."*
> *Proverbs 3:5-6, NKJV*

## Group Discussion

1.      Describe the comfort you receive knowing that God doesn't change.

2.      Describe the role of faith in overcoming the fear of change.

3.      Describe any areas in your own life that you've been reluctant to change.

---

[1] Johnson, Spencer. Who Moved My Cheese? New York; Putnam Penguin, 1998.

[2] Biblesoft's New Exhaustive Strong's Numbers and Concordance with Expanded Greek-Hebrew Dictionary. Copyright © 1994, 2003 Biblesoft, Inc. and International Bible Translators, Inc.

[3] Thayer's Greek Lexicon, Electronic Database. Copyright (c) 2000 by Biblesoft

# Personal Notes

# Fear Factors
# Peace & Love

Ever made these statements? *"I'm so worried . . ." That just worries me to death . . ." "I've always been a worry wart . . ."* Fear, anxiety, phobias begin in our thoughts and are confirmed in our words. It's no wonder that in one of the classic passages on worry, Jesus said, *"So do not worry, saying . . ."* If you want your fear factors to multiply, just start *saying* all the things you are afraid, anxious and phobic about! God wants our minds to be free from anxiety, worry and cares. If we don't take control of our thoughts, they become imaginations; if we don't take control of our imagination they become strongholds. You can tell if you have a stronghold of fear, anxiety or phobias in your life by listening to yourself! Do you find yourself saying things like, *"I'm so scared. Well, you know me, I'm just all nerved up. That's just the way I am!"* Is that the way "you" are? Is that the way God wants you to be? God wants your life full of His peace and His love which will drive out fear, anxiety and phobias. Really! If we will give God's Word our attention, He will replace our fears with His peace and love.

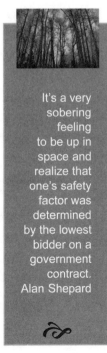

**☞Nugget☜** Are you a world class "worrier" and proud of it? Perhaps you would be insulted to hear that worry is not a godly quality. Often worriers rationalize their worry by saying this is just their way of showing love and concern for their loved ones. After all, how can a mother not worry? How can a business man or stock trader not worry? Jesus said it was possible to live worry free; to live care free! Actually, habitual worriers are in bondage. Worry and anxiety has become such a strong hold in their minds that they believe this is "just the way they are," and in reality these worriers are disobeying the Lord's command to not worry!

It's a very sobering feeling to be up in space and realize that one's safety factor was determined by the lowest bidder on a government contract.
Alan Shepard

Peace of mind is God's plan. He wants us to live in a state of peace and He's provided the way for that to be a reality in our lives. Are you ready to be honest? Let's make this our prayer as we look at the fear factors, peace and love. *"Search me, O God, and know my heart; try me, and know my anxieties; 24 And see if there is any wicked way in me, and lead me in the way everlasting."* Psalm 139:23-24, NKJV

## No Worries, Mon

This is what they say in Jamaica and this ought to be the confession of faith for every Christian!

1.      Proverbs 12:25

Underline the words "anxiety," "depression," "good word" and "glad."

*Anxiety in the heart of man causes depression, but a good word makes it glad. NKJV*

Where does anxiety try to lodge itself? _____

What is the result of anxiety? _____

_____

If you want your heart to be happy, what does it need to hear? _____

_____

What good words can you begin saying today? _____

_____

2.      Luke 10:41-42

Underline Martha's problem.

*38 As Jesus and his disciples were on their way, he came to a village where a woman named Martha opened her home to him. 39 She had a sister called Mary, who sat at the Lord's feet listening to what he said. 40 But Martha was distracted by all the preparations that had to be made. She came to him and asked, "Lord, don't you care that my sister has left me to do the work by myself? Tell her to help me!" 41 "Martha, Martha," the Lord answered, "you are worried and upset about many things, 42 but only one thing is needed. Mary has chosen what is better, and it will not be taken away from her. NIV*

Martha lived the life many of us live.

According to verses 40 and 41, what was Martha worried about? _____

_____

What did Mary do? _____

Who did Jesus say chose the most important thing? _____

Do you think that Mary's choice to sit at Jesus' feet kept her free from worry and anxiety? How?

_____

In what ways do you find that spending time with the Lord keeps you free from worry and anxiety?

_____

_____

෧**Nugget**෧    Like many of you, I can relate to Martha. If you're a "Type A" personality you understand the need for speed, accomplishment, and being a "get ur done" type of person. Have you figured out that there will always be things to do? Your checklist will never get done! Your desk will never be uncluttered. The house will not stay clean. The weeds will grow. People will always demand things of you. That's life and it's very likely that it's not going to slow down. So, that means we have to find God's peace in the midst of schedules, deadlines, stress, checklists, demands, life, marriage, parenting and work. The only place we'll find God's peace is in His Presence! Sitting at His feet—reading His Word, worshipping Him, praying and casting all our cares on Him—that's the place we receive His peace.

3.      Philippians 4:6-9

Underline the words that describe what we are supposed to think about.

*6 Do not be anxious about anything, but in everything, by prayer and petition, with thanksgiving, present your requests to God. 7 And the peace of God, which transcends all understanding, will guard your hearts and your minds in Christ Jesus. 8 Finally, brothers, whatever is true, whatever is noble, whatever is right, whatever is pure, whatever is lovely, whatever is admirable-if anything is excellent or praiseworthy-think about such things. 9 Whatever you have learned or received or heard from me, or seen in me-put it into practice. And the God of peace will be with you. NIV*

What are we allowed to be anxious or worried about? _____

According to verse 6, what is the remedy for anxiety? _____

What does God give our hearts and minds to wash anxiety away? _____

_____

To live anxiety-free, our thoughts must be focused on what things?

_____

4. Matthew 6:25-34

Underline the things we are not to worry about.

*25 Therefore I tell you, do not worry about your life, what you will eat or drink; or about your body, what you will wear. Is not life more important than food, and the body more important than clothes? 26 Look at the birds of the air; they do not sow or reap or store away in barns, and yet your heavenly Father feeds them. Are you not much more valuable than they? 27 Who of you by worrying can add a single hour to his life? 28 "And why do you worry about clothes? See how the lilies of the field grow. They do not labor or spin. 29 Yet I tell you that not even Solomon in all his splendor was dressed like one of these. 30 If that is how God clothes the grass of the field, which is here today and tomorrow is thrown into the fire, will he not much more clothe you, O you of little faith? 31 So do not worry, saying, 'What shall we eat?' or 'What shall we drink?' or 'What shall we wear?' 32 For the pagans run after all these things, and your heavenly Father knows that you need them. 33 But seek first his kingdom and his righteousness, and all these things will be given to you as well. 34 Therefore do not worry about tomorrow, for tomorrow will worry about itself. Each day has enough trouble of its own. NIV*

If we are not to worry about our life, our food or drink, our body or our clothes, what kind of life would that give us?

_____

Which of these areas are you most tempted to worry about?

_____

_____

If God be our God, He will give us peace in trouble. When there is a storm without, He will make peace within. The world can create trouble in peace, but God can create peace in trouble.
Thomas Watson

How do verses 26-30 bring comfort and peace to our minds? _____

_____

Rather than worry, what should we seek first?

_____

What does God promise us? _____

_____

What are you tempted to worry about? _____

☙**Nugget**❧ Years ago the Lord gave me a little song that has helped me over the years. When I am feeling stressed I just sing this little ditty and find His peace. The song is titled, "Resting In Your Presence."

*I am resting in Your Presence*
*I'm relaxed when I'm with You*
*There's no need to worry*
*About the things I have to do*

*No more toiling*
*No more striving*
*I've decided not to spin*
*I'm finally realizing, efforts in my flesh are sin.*

Perhaps the Lord has a song for you. As you get quiet and listen to your heart, see if the Lord has put some encouraging words of peace in your heart and if so, sing it out! You'll find great peace!

5.      1 Peter 5:7

Underline the words that describe God's heart.

*Cast all your anxiety on him because he cares for you. NIV*

Which of our cares or anxieties should we cast on the Lord? _____

How do you cast your cares on the Lord? _____

_____

What is God's heart toward you? _____

## Peace, Out!

The answer to anxiety and worry is peace. God gives us a peace that passes our understanding—our anxieties and worries—and this peace is found in Him. Let's look at it.

1.      Psalm 29:11

Underline the words that describe the things the Lord wants to give His people.

*The LORD will give strength unto his people; the LORD will bless his people with peace. KJV*

Is peace and strength God's will for you? _____

Do you believe it? _____

2.      Psalm 37:37

Underline the word that describes God's desire for His followers.

*Mark the perfect man, and behold the upright: for the end of that man is peace. KJV*

In your own words, what does it mean to be "perfect" and "upright"?

_____

3.      Psalm 119:165

Underline the word that describes the type of peace the Lord wants us to have.

*Great peace have those who love Your law, and nothing causes them to stumble. NKJV*

Who gets "great peace"? _____

Do you love God's Word in this way? _____

4.      Proverbs 3:1-2

Underline the result of keeping God's Word in the midst of your heart.

*1 My son, do not forget my law, but let your heart keep my commands; 2 For length of days and long life and peace they will add to you. NKJV*

If you keep God's Word real in your heart and life, what does it bring you?

_____

5.      Proverbs 3:13-18

Underline the results for those who seek wisdom.

*13 Happy is the man who finds wisdom, and the man who gains understanding; 14 For her proceeds are better than the profits of silver, and her gain than fine gold. 15 She is more precious than rubies, and all the things you may desire cannot compare with her. 16 Length of days is in her right hand, in her left hand riches and honor. 17 Her ways are ways of pleasantness, and all her paths are peace. 18 She is a tree of life to those who take hold of her, and happy are all who retain her. NKJV*

If you want your life to profit, last long, be pleasant, peaceful and full of life, what must you retain?

_____

6.  John 14:27

Underline the word "peace."

*Peace I leave with you; my peace I give you. I do not give to you as the world gives. Do not let your hearts be troubled and do not be afraid. NIV*

If we want to have Jesus' peace, what must we not allow our hearts to do?

_____

This is sometimes seemingly difficult. What are some ways you stop your heart from being "troubled"?

_____

7.  John 16:33

Underline the place we find peace.
*I have told you these things, so that in me you may have peace. In this world you will have trouble. But take heart! I have overcome the world. NIV*

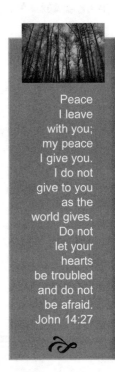

Peace I leave with you; my peace I give you. I do not give to you as the world gives. Do not let your hearts be troubled and do not be afraid.
John 14:27

What did Jesus say we would have in this world? _____

Where do we find peace? _____

8.     2 Peter 1:2

Underline the two things God wants multiplied in your life.

*Grace and peace be multiplied to you in the knowledge of God and of Jesus our Lord . . . NKJV*

How does God multiply grace and peace for you? _____

_____

The more you get to know God the more grace and peace are multiplied to you!

## Peace Of Mind

1.     Isaiah 26:3

Underline the word that describes God's peace.

*You will keep him in perfect peace, whose mind is stayed on You, because he trusts in You. NKJV*

What does it mean to have your mind "stayed on God"? _____

_____

What is the result of keeping your mind stayed on God and your trust in Him?

_____

2.  Philippians 4:4-7

Underline the words "anything" and "everything."

*4 Rejoice in the Lord always. I will say it again: Rejoice! 5 Let your gentleness be evident to all. The Lord is near. 6 Do not be anxious about anything, but in everything, by prayer and petition, with thanksgiving, present your requests to God. 7 And the peace of God, which transcends all understanding, will guard your hearts and your minds in Christ Jesus. 8 Finally, brothers, whatever is true, whatever is noble, whatever is right, whatever is pure, whatever is lovely, whatever is admirable-if anything is excellent or praiseworthy-think about such things. 9 Whatever you have learned or received or heard from me, or seen in me-put it into practice. And the God of peace will be with you. NIV*

In what things does God allow us to be anxious? _____

What do we need to do if we want the peace that passes all understanding?

_____

3.  Colossians 3:15

Underline the word "rule."

*Let the peace of Christ rule in your hearts . . . NIV*

Where does God want peace to rule? _____

❧**Nugget**❧  Did you know that you can have peace in your heart, while anxiety and worry try to tempt your mind? God wants you to let peace win! Make anxiety and worry obey the peace that is ruling in your heart.

I love the way the Amplified Bible describes this verse: *"And let the peace (soul harmony which comes) from Christ rule (act as umpire continually) in your hearts [deciding and settling with finality all questions that arise in your minds, in that peaceful state] to which as [members of Christ's] one body you were also called [to live]. And be thankful (appreciative), [giving praise to God always]." AMP*

4.      Psalm 119:165

Underline the phrase "great peace" and "love Your law".

*Great peace have those who love Your law . . .*

If you want great peace, what should you love? _____

The best thing you can do to bring peace to your mind and heart is feed on the Word of God! Read it. Ponder it. Soak in it. Marinate in it. Saturate your mind with the Word and you will experience great peace.

## Perfect Love Casts Out Fear

When we begin to understand the incredible depth of God's love for us, we are able to live in the peace that passes all understanding. Fear cannot exist where God's peace abides! Let's look at it.

1.      1 John 4:18

Underline the words "fear" and "love."

*There is no fear in love; but perfect love casts out fear, because fear involves torment. But he who fears has not been made perfect in love. NKJV*

Just as I had to trust in the "harness man" holding on to the rope as I climbed the wall, we have to trust in God's love for us.

Fear cannot exist where? _____

What does perfect love do? _____

If we struggle with fear, what do we need to be more established in? _____

_____

2.      Romans 8:35-39

Underline the phrase "we are more than conquerors through Him."

*35 Who shall separate us from the love of Christ? Shall tribulation, or distress, or persecution, or famine, or nakedness, or peril, or sword? 36 As it is written: "For Your sake we are killed all day long; we are accounted as sheep for the slaughter." 37 Yet in all these things we are more than conquerors through Him who loved us. 38 For I am persuaded that neither death nor life, nor angels nor principalities nor powers, nor things present nor things to come, 39 nor height nor depth, nor any other created thing, shall be able to separate us from the love of God which is in Christ Jesus our Lord. NKJV*

God loves us. It's a fact.

Can anything separate us from His love? _____

List all the things in verses 35, 38 and 39 that could generate fear. _____

_____

Verse 37 tells us the bottom line: what does God's Word promise us?

_____

## Scriptures To Chew On

Taking time to meditate on and memorize God's Word is invaluable. Hiding His Word in our hearts will strengthen us for the present and arm us for the future. Here are two verses to memorize and chew on this week. Write these verses on index cards and carry them with you this week. If you will post them in your bathroom, dashboard, desk, locker or other convenient places, you will find these Scriptures taking root in your heart.

*"Great peace have those who love Your law . . . "*
*Psalm 119:165, NKJV*

*"I've told you all this so that trusting me,*
*you will be unshakable and assured, deeply at peace.*
*In this godless world you will continue to experience difficulties.*
*But take heart! I've conquered the world."*
*John 16:33, The Message*

## Group Discussion

1.  Describe the things you say when it comes to fear, anxiety and phobias. Are your words working for you or against you?

2.  Which three verses on God's peace ministered to you?

3.  Describe how and why God's perfect love casts out fear.

## Fear Factors
## Faith & Courage

If you've ever watched *Fear Factor* on TV, perhaps you've noticed that while these contestants are trying to overcome their greatest fears and win the competition, they often develop an attitude. Their cocky, obnoxious attitudes are often over exaggerated in the hope that they will intimidate their opponents and win! Apparently, the 'tude helps them find a certain degree of courage and faith to win.

Overcoming anxiety, fear and phobias in life is not a game show competition, but it does require us to develop an attitude. We need to develop a faith-and-courage-filled attitude that will intimidate our opponent. Are you ready to get a little 'tude? Let's see what God's Word says about this.

## Jesus Told Us To Fear Not

Jesus told us to fear not, but rather to trust in Him. Is that possible? Let's look at it.

1.    Mark 4:35-5:1

       Underline the words that Jesus said in verse 35.
       Underline the fulfillment of Jesus' words in verse 5:1.

       *35 On the same day, when evening had come, He said to them, "Let us cross over to the other side." 36 Now when they had left the multitude, they took Him along in the boat as He was. And other little boats were also with Him. 37 And a great*

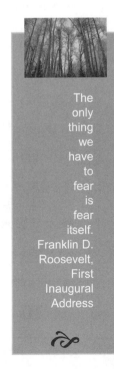

The only thing we have to fear is fear itself.
Franklin D. Roosevelt, First Inaugural Address

*windstorm arose, and the waves beat into the boat, so that it was
already filling. 38 But He was in the stern, asleep on a pillow. And they
awoke Him and said to Him, "Teacher, do You not care that we are
perishing?" 39 Then He arose and rebuked the wind, and said to the
sea, "Peace, be still!" And the wind ceased and there was a great calm.
40 But He said to them, "Why are you so fearful? How is it that you
have no faith?" 41 And they feared exceedingly, and said to one another,
"Who can this be, that even the wind and the sea obey Him!" 5:1 Then
they came to the other side of the sea, to the country of the Gadarenes.
NKJV*

What did Jesus tell his disciples in verse 35? _____

Jesus declared His will in verse 35, and then in verse 37 the
circumstances looked contrary to what Jesus had declared.

What happened? _____

In verse 38, what did the disciples ask? _____

In verse 40, what did Jesus ask? _____

What do you think Jesus meant regarding the relationship between fear
and faith?

_____

Anytime we begin to question whether the Lord cares about us or not,
it's a signal that we are not resting in His love. Instead, fear and unbelief
are trying to take over our mental, emotional and spiritual lives.

In chapter 5, verse 1, what was the end result of Jesus' original
statement?

_____

⊱Nugget⊰ When we take God at His Word, He will deliver. Jesus said, "Let's go to the other side" and sure enough, they landed at the "other side." They faced a storm in between the promise and the fulfillment of that promise, just as we often do. The important thing is to ask ourselves, how will we handle circumstances, weather, winds, economies, symptoms, situations that look contrary to what God has promised? Will we stay in faith or will we allow fear to dominate?

2.      Matthew 14:24-27

Underline the words that describe Jesus' reaction to the disciples fear.

*25 At about four o'clock in the morning, Jesus came toward them walking on the water. 26 They were scared out of their wits. "A ghost!" they said, crying out in terror. 27 But Jesus was quick to comfort them. "Courage, it's me. Don't be afraid." The Message*

Here's another scary situation. Have you ever seen a ghost, walking on water at 4 in the morning?

How does verse 26 describe the disciples? _____

In verse 27, how did Jesus comfort them? _____

⊱Nugget⊰ I think it's interesting that while Jesus comforts us with His words, He doesn't cuddle and coo us when we are afraid. He simply says, *"Fear not! Be not afraid."* It's His command. Yes, the circumstances were something anyone would be freaked out by in the natural. Nonetheless, Jesus said, *"Don't be afraid!"* When the winds are blowing, waves are crashing in on your boat and it looks like you are about to sink, you'd think that Jesus would say something like, *"Oh, come here you sweet little baby. Oh, bless your heart. It's kinda scary, isn't it? You poor thing, I know this is hard on your faith . . ."* But notice that Jesus never does that. Rather, He jerks the slack out of the disciples (and us) and says as a matter of fact, *"Fear not!" "Don't be afraid."* He rebukes them for having small faith by asking them, *"Where is your faith?"* It's as if He expected them to live free from fear! This is where the attitude comes in—if you'll pardon the expression this is where as a Christian you have to set your face like flint toward God and His Word come hell or high water.

Obviously, it is wise to have healthy respect for and exercise wise caution in certain settings of evil and danger. For example, it's healthy to avoid putting your hand on a hot stove for "fear" of getting burned; it's wise to wear a hard hat in a construction zone for "fear" of falling objects. However, fear, anxiety and worry are unhealthy and unwise in most arenas of life because they are tools of the enemy to trip up and paralyze believers. Sixty-three times the King James Version of the Bible tells us to "fear not", 28 times the KJV tells us to "be not afraid", 13 times the New International Version of the Bible tells us, "do not worry", and 11 times the NIV talks to us about anxiety or being anxious. Over and over, the Lord tells us that fear, anxiety and worry are to have no place in our lives.

3.      Job 3:25-26

Circle the words "feared" and "dreaded."

*25 What I feared has come upon me; what I dreaded has happened to me. 26 I have no peace, no quietness; I have no rest, but only turmoil. NIV*

☞**Nugget**☜ Many people don't understand the book of Job. Often, they blame God for allowing such tragedy to happen to Job and they just hope and pray they aren't the next Job! Job was a righteous man; one of the best "Christians" of his day, yet while Job loved God, he lived in fear. What Job greatly feared came upon him. Fear can attract the very thing it advertises. Faith in God and His Word brings forth good things. Fear in the devil and his deceit often brings forth bad things. While we will not do an in-depth study in the book of Job and all the reasons, why's and how's of his life, we do see a classic example of the product of fear in Job's life.

What did Job say—with his own words—had come upon him? _____

_____

Fear and dread work hand in hand.

In addition to the severe consequences Job faced, the result of fear and dread produced what type of mental, emotional and spiritual life for Job, according to verse 26?

_____

Let's look at Biblical factors to overcoming fear.

## Faith and Courage

The following verses of Scripture show us how to have faith and courage in the midst of fear. When we take God at His Word, He shows Himself strong on our behalf. When we operate in fear rather than faith, we limit God's ability in our lives and we don't enter the place of quietness, rest and freedom from fear. Let's look at God's Word to see what we can learn about faith and courage.

1. Deuteronomy 31:6

   Underline the phrases "be strong and of good courage" and "fear not."

   *Be strong and of a good courage, fear not, nor be afraid of them: for the LORD thy God, he it is that doth go with thee; he will not fail thee, nor forsake thee. KJV*

   What four things are we told to do? _____

   _____

Courage is not the absence of fear, but rather the judgement that something else is more important than fear.
Ambrose Redmoon

What is courage? _____

What three things are we told that the Lord will do? _____

_____

How does knowing this about the Lord help you to stay free from fear?

_____

If God said *"Be strong and of a good courage"* and *"Fear not, nor be afraid"*, we must have the ability to obey Him, right?

2.      Joshua 1:6-9

Underline the words that describe faith and courage.

*6 Be strong and of good courage, for to this people you shall divide as an inheritance the land which I swore to their fathers to give them. 7 Only be strong and very courageous, that you may observe to do according to all the law which Moses My servant commanded you; do not turn from it to the right hand or to the left, that you may prosper wherever you go. 8 This Book of the Law shall not depart from your mouth, but you shall meditate in it day and night, that you may observe to do according to all that is written in it. For then you will make your way prosperous, and then you will have good success. 9 Have I not commanded you? Be strong and of good courage; do not be afraid, nor be dismayed, for the LORD your God is with you wherever you go. NKJV*

God's people were facing some enemies as they pursued their inheritance of the Promised Land.

In verses 6, 7 and 9, what did the Lord command? _____

_____

⬧**Nugget**⬧ Notice that being strong, courageous and fearless is commanded. It's as if God expects us to have the ability to live free from fear! It's not a suggestion or a helpful hint, it's a command! If God commands it, is it possible? Of course! Although we may not "feel" courageous or fearless, it is possible to overcome our feelings and choose by faith to be courageous, strong and fearless!

In verses 8 and 9, we get the secret to living the fear free, successful, blessed life. What four things are we told to do?

_____

_____

3.      Luke 8:41-56

Underline all the words of Jesus.

*41 Then a man named Jairus, a ruler of the synagogue, came and fell at Jesus' feet, pleading with him to come to his house 42 because his only daughter, a girl of about twelve, was dying. As Jesus was on his way, the crowds almost crushed him. 43 And a woman was there who had been subject to bleeding for twelve years, but no one could heal her. 44 She came up behind him and touched the edge of his cloak, and immediately her bleeding stopped. 45 "Who touched me?" Jesus asked. When they all denied it, Peter said, "Master, the people are crowding and pressing against you." 46 But Jesus said, "Someone touched me; I know that power has gone out from me." 47 Then the woman, seeing that she could not go unnoticed, came trembling and fell at his feet. In the presence of all the people, she told why she had touched him and how she had been instantly healed. 48 Then he said to her, "Daughter, your faith has healed you. Go in peace." 49 While Jesus was still speaking, someone came from the house of Jairus, the synagogue ruler. "Your daughter is dead," he said. "Don't bother the teacher any more." 50 Hearing this, Jesus said to Jairus, "Don't be afraid; just believe, and she will be healed." 51 When he arrived at the house of Jairus, he did not let anyone go in with him except Peter, John and James, and the child's father and mother. 52 Meanwhile, all the people were wailing and mourning for her. "Stop wailing," Jesus said. "She is not dead but asleep." 53 They laughed at him, knowing that she was dead. 54 But he took her by the hand and said, "My child, get up!" 55 Her spirit returned, and at once she stood up. Then Jesus told them to give her something to eat. 56 Her parents were astonished, but he ordered them not to tell anyone what had happened. NIV*

What fearful situation did Jairus face? _____

In verses 43-48, who interrupted Jairus' plea for Jesus' help? _____

_____

Sometimes it seems that other things come in to interrupt our need for God's help. It's important that we keep our eyes on the Lord, even when it looks like our prayer for help has been interrupted.

In verse 49, a bad situation got worse. Someone from Jairus' house spoke words that would certainly fill a father's heart with fear and grief. What did Jairus hear?

_____

In verse 50, Jesus immediately spoke words that would fill Jairus' heart with faith. What did Jesus say?

_____

Have you ever had to choose between the words of others (bankers, doctors, lawyers, TV commentators, friends, family, pastors, etc.) and the words of Jesus?

_____

What was the result of faith in Jesus words? _____

What do you think would have happened if Jairus had given in to fear, anxiety and worry?

_____

≫**Nugget**≫ We need faith to overcome fear. God's Word is the only thing that gives us the solid faith we need to overcome fear. Romans 10:17 tells us, "... *faith comes by hearing, and hearing by the word of God.*" *NKJV* If you want faith to come into your life, it only comes by hearing God's Word. Faith doesn't come by wishing for it, begging for it, crying for it or even by praying for it. Faith comes as we hear God's Word and His Words take preeminence over all other words. When we place our faith in God's Word, it becomes an anchor for our soul and causes us to overcome the temptation to place our faith in fear-filled words or reports. Just as Jairus had the choice to make between believing Jesus' words or the words of his circumstances, we also have to make that choice. Faith in God's Word requires that we know His Word. By studying God's Word, we can know God's will for us. We must study and meditate on His Word so when the winds blow, the bad reports come in, and the devil huffs and puffs, we can stand strong and courageous in the Word of God.

## The Spirit of Faith

Not only does God want us to have faith, He wants us to have the "spirit of faith"! What is the spirit of faith? The spirit of faith is seen in the person who is sold out on filling their heart with God's Word and speaking those very words with their mouth. They make sure that their heart and mouth agree with God and His Word. You won't find a person with the spirit of faith speaking doubt, unbelief and fear-filled talk, but rather they choose to believe God and His Word and that's what they speak about. When fear,

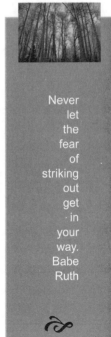

Never let the fear of striking out get in your way. Babe Ruth

danger, tragedy, calamities and terror try to intimidate, scare, panic or send them into fear, the person with the spirit of faith will respond with faith in God and His Word. You'll find a person that believes God can be trusted. His Word is more true than any circumstance and they will take it to the bank! The spirit of faith is tangible. You can sense it in a church. You can hear it in a person's words. You can see it in action in the time of trouble. What does the Bible say about the spirit of faith?

1.      2 Corinthians 4:13-14

Underline the phrases "spirit of faith," "I believed" and "I have spoken."

*It is written: "I believed; therefore I have spoken." With that same spirit of faith we also believe and therefore speak . . . NIV*

What two components make up the spirit of faith? _____

_____

_____

Do you have the spirit of faith? _____

2.      Romans 10:8-10

Underline the phrases "the word of faith," "confess with your mouth" and "believe in your heart."

*8 But what does it say? "The word is near you; it is in your mouth and in your heart," that is, the word of faith we are proclaiming: 9 That if you confess with your mouth, "Jesus is Lord," and believe in your heart that God raised him from the dead, you will be saved. 10 For it is with your heart that you believe and are justified, and it is with your mouth that you confess and are saved. NIV*

What two components make up the "word of faith"? _____

_____

In this passage, how important are both "believing in the heart" and "confessing with your mouth" as it relates to salvation?

_____

_____

Can you see that if we are going to live by the Word of faith and have the spirit of faith, we are going to have to discipline our heart and mouth to agree with and speak God's Word?

## The Only Acceptable Fear

Finally, there is one Person we *should* fear: God. It's healthy to revere and fear Him and Him alone. To fear the Lord is to reverence Him. Having reverence for God implies that we esteem Him and His Words; that we obey Him, serve Him, worship Him. It does not mean to live in dread of the Lord in the sense that we cower and run from Him, but rather that we run to Him out of respect and reverence.

1.      Proverbs 1:7, 9:10 and Psalm 111:10

        Underline the phrase "the fear of the Lord."

        *1:7 The fear of the LORD is the beginning of knowledge . . . NKJV*

        *9:10 The fear of the LORD is the beginning of wisdom . . . NKJV*

        *111:10 The fear of the LORD is the beginning of wisdom; a good understanding have all those who do His commandments. His praise endures forever. NKJV*

What do these verses tell us begins when we walk in the fear of the Lord?

_____

2.  Proverbs 14:26

Underline the phrase "the fear of the Lord."

_In the fear of the LORD there is strong confidence . . . NKJV_

When we fear the Lord, what do we walk in? _____

3.  Proverbs 14:27

Underline the phrase "the fear of the Lord."

_The fear of the LORD is a fountain of life, to turn one away from the snares of death. NKJV_

What does the "fear of the Lord" bring to your life? _____

What does the "fear of the Lord" keep away from your life? _____

_____

4.  Proverbs 19:23

Underline the phrase "the fear of the Lord."

_The fear of the LORD leads to life, and he who has it will abide in satisfaction; He will not be visited with evil. NKJV_

The fear of the Lord will lead to what? _____

The fear of the Lord will cause you to abide in what? _____

The fear of the Lord will keep you from what type of visitor? _____

How do you fear the Lord? _____

_____

&**Nugget**&> To walk in the fear of the Lord is to have a healthy respect and reverence for God. It does not mean that we are afraid of Him, but rather we desire to live a life worthy of the Lord fully pleasing to Him. We recognize that He is God Almighty, the Most High, and above Him there is no other. He is the Potter and we are the clay. He is the Creator and we are His creation. We choose to live a life that seeks to know Him, please Him and glorify Him in all that we do.

I pray that this Bite Sized Bible Study helped give you more knowledge, wisdom and practical tools that will help you live in freedom from anxiety, fear and phobias.

May this be your testimony . . .

"I sought the LORD, and he answered me;
he delivered me from all my fears."
Psalm 34:4, NIV

## Scriptures To Chew On

Taking time to meditate on and memorize God's Word is invaluable. Hiding His Word in our hearts will strengthen us for the present and arm us for the future. Here are two verses to memorize and chew on this week. Write these verses on index cards and carry them with you this week. If you will post them in your bathroom, dashboard, desk, locker or other convenient places, you will find these Scriptures taking root in your heart.

"For God has not given us a spirit of fear,
but of power and of love and of a sound mind."
2 Timothy 1:7, NKJV

*"I sought the LORD, and He heard me,*
*And delivered me from all my fears."*
Psalm 34:4, NKJV

# Group Discussion

1.  Describe the idea that God commands us to "Fear not." What does that mean in your life?

2.  Describe a time in your life when you have had to choose courage over fear.

3.  Describe the importance of having the "spirit of faith."

# Personal Notes

# The "Bite Sized Bible Study Series"
## By Beth Jones

*When your words came, I ate them;*
*they were my joy and my heart's delight . . .*
*Jeremiah 15:16 NIV*

- Six practical Bible studies for Christians living in today's culture.
- Each book contains 6 sessions designed for individual & small group study.
- Great studies targeting men, women, believers and seekers of all ages.
- Convenient size 6" x 9", each book is between 80-144 pages.
- Fill-in-the-blank book with Group Discussion questions after each session.
- "Nuggets" throughout each study explain Scriptures in easy to follow way.
- Written in a contemporary style using practical illustrations.
- Perfect for small group curriculum, bookstores and churches.

## Satisfied Lives For Desperate Housewives
*God's Word On Proverbs 31*
**Great Study For Women, Retail $7.99**
**ISBN: 1-933433-04-3**

Session 1: Desperate For God
Session 2: Desperate For Balance
Session 3: Desperate For A Great Marriage
Session 4: Desperate For Godly Kids
Session 5: Desperate To Serve
Session 6: Desperate For Purpose

## Grace For The Pace
*God's Word For Stressed & Overloaded Lives*
**Great Study For Men & Women, Retail $7.99**
**ISBN: 1-933433-02-7**

Session 1: Escape From Hamsterville
Session 2: Help Is Here
Session 3: How Do You Spell Relief?
Session 4: Get A Bigger Frying Pan
Session 5: Houston, We Have A Problem!
Session 6: Time Keeps On Ticking

## Call Or Go Online To Order:
## 800-596-0379
## www.valleypresspublishers.com

# Kissed Or Dissed

*God's Word For Feeling Rejected & Overlooked*
**Great Study For Women, Retail $7.99**
**ISBN: 1-933433-01-9**

Session 1: Dissed 101
Session 2: Blessed & Highly Favored
Session 3: Edit Your Life
Session 4: That's What I'm Talking About
Session 5: Sow Acceptance Seeds
Session 6: Just Like Jesus

# What To Do When You Feel Blue

*God's Word For Depression & Discouragement*
**Great Study For Men & Women, Retail $7.99**
**ISBN: 1-933433-00-0**

Session 1: When The Sky Is Not Blue
Session 2: No Pity Parties Allowed
Session 3: The Things You Could Think
Session 4: Go To Your Happy Place
Session 5: You've Got To Have Friends
Session 6: Lift Up The Down

# The Friends God Sends

*God's Word On Friendship & Chick Chat*
**Great Study For Women, Retail $7.99**
**ISBN: 1-933433-05-1**

Session 1: Friendship Realities
Session 2: The Friendship Workout
Session 3: God-Knit Friendships
Session 4: Who's On Your Boat?
Session 5: Anatomy of A Friendship Famine
Session 6: A Friend of God

# Don't Factor Fear Here

*God's Word For Overcoming Anxiety, Fear & Phobias*
**Great Study For Men & Women, Retail $7.99**
**ISBN: 1-933433-03-5**

Session 1: Fear of Death
Session 2: Fear of Man
Session 3: Fear of Danger
Session 4: Fear of Change
Session 5: Fear Factors - Love & Peace
Session 6: Fear Factors - Faith & Courage

# Why The Gory, Bloody Details?
## By Beth Jones

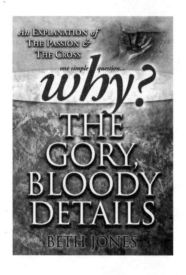

. . . right before
your very eyes–
Jesus Christ
(the Messiah)
was openly
and graphically
set forth
and
portrayed
as crucified . . .
Galatians 3:1, AMP

### Why The Gory, Bloody Details?
### An Explanation of the Passion and the Cross

Retail Paperback $4.99, Hardcover $7.99

ISBN: 0-9717156-6-1 Paperback
ISBN: 0-9717156-7-X Hardcover

This contagious 96-page giftbook answers the basic question, "Why did Jesus have to die on the cross?" People want to know: Why did Jesus endure such brutality? Why did God allow His own Son to be murdered? Why the gore and blood? It's a great evangelistic gift for unsaved friends and family and a great educational resource for believers who want to understand the cross and the passion.

- *Evangelistic gift book explains the cross—perfect for seekers.*
- *Gospel presented in a relevant, easy to understand way.*
- *Gift book size 4" x 6", 96 pages.*
- *Written in a contemporary style using practical illustrations.*
- *Hardcover and paperback.*

ALLEY PRESS
PUBLISHERS

A Ministry of Kalamazoo Valley Family Church
995 Romence Road
Portage, MI 49024
Ph. 800-596-0379
www.valleypresspublishers.com

# Beth**Jones**.org

a

simple

casual

blog

articles

and

bible

studies

topics

like

eternal life

girl stuff

healing

ministry

finances

holy spirit

prayer

victory

faq

click

it

.